FREE ENTERPRISE

and

THE ADMINISTRATIVE STATE

FREE
ENTERPRISE
and
THE ADMINISTRATIVE STATE

MARSHALL E. DIMOCK

GREENWOOD PRESS, PUBLISHERS
WESTPORT, CONNECTICUT

The Library of Congress has catalogued this publication as follows:

Library of Congress Cataloging in Publication Data

Dimock, Marshall Edward, 1903–
   Free enterprise and the administrative state.

   Includes bibliographical references.
   1. Capitalism. 2. State, The. 3. United States—
Economic policy. I. Title.
HB501.D525 1972   330.12'2   76-142856
ISBN 0-8371-5955-5

Copyright 1951 by University of Alabama Press

Originally published in 1951 by University of Alabama Press,
University, Alabama

Reprinted with the permission of University of Alabama Press

First Greenwood Reprinting 1972

Library of Congress Catalogue Card Number 76-142856

ISBN 0-8371-5955-5

Printed in the United States of America

PREFACE

THERE ARE SEVERAL ways of viewing the free enterprise system. It is, for example, the "natural" system, based on the dictates of the impersonal market, and as such, the less there is of human interference and decision-making, the better it will function and the more everyone will be benefited. Or the free enterprise system may be regarded as a high level abstraction employed by skilled propagandists to cultivate predetermined attitudes toward ownership and liberty on the part of the public.

There is, however, still another way of viewing the free enterprise system, and that is from the standpoint of institutions, how they are organized, how they behave, and how they are managed. This view, which is in the ascendency among a growing number of economists, is the one that will be taken in the present five essays. This is the pragmatic, the realistic approach. The free enterprise system then becomes a subject of scientific inquiry, the product of cause-and-effect relationships growing out of human and institutional activities as well as a system of goal-values. Such a combination makes it more meaningful and more readily defended and improved because when problems arise in its functioning, it is possible to discover how they arose and what, if anything, can be done to correct them.

The practical solution of practical problems involves a careful, systematic analysis of cause-and-effect relationships, an assertion that is coming to be almost as widely accepted in the marts of trade as in the cloistered halls of learning. In the present essays the center of interest is the overlap between the administrative process and the relations of business and government. Here a new regrouping of data is taking place and a redoubling of effort is occurring, marking a general line of development which holds great promise in terms of its effect on practical solutions secured through logical processes.

Institutions bulk so large in our community life today that it is natural for administrative theory to forge to the center. That it has been doing so in recent years is attested in many ways, not the least promising of which is the appearance of such volumes as Elton Mayo's *Social Problems of an Industrial Civilization* and Alexander Leighton's *The Governing of Men*. They have in common a broadening and deepening of administrative theory to include all essential elements of the compound. In so doing they make administration more realistic and more able to solve the complex institutional problems that press in on us.

If there were such a thing as a general theory of social science (and there is, no doubt, but it has yet to be fully developed), it would be found that administrative theory occupies a central position in almost every important problem encountered. This is inevitable because group relationships and institutional operation dominate modern society and an explanation of the how and why of their operation is administrative theory.

Formal economics also may be expected increasingly to reflect the importance of administrative theory. The theoretical and the institutional are not two separate and exclusive approaches to economics. Older opinion to the contrary, this dichotomy is insupportable because institutional behavior also is based on an important underlying theory. The problem, therefore, is not one of reconciling two separate approaches but of absorbing administrative theory into general economic theory. Amongst younger economists this view is already widely held. Thus economics may be expected increasingly to draw from political science and political science will recognize, and act upon, its close relationship to economics. Administrative theory is the catalytic agent helping to bring this transformation about.

In the present volume a series of basic and related problems is dealt with. The subject of the first essay is the free enterprise system, what it is and what causes it to change. The conclusion drawn is that a knowledge of institutional dynamics and administrative theory has more to do with the survival of that system (or any other) than the reinforcing of uncritical belief systems. Next comes the problem of monopoly and the antitrust laws, where, again, administrative factors are found to be at the center of any lasting solution. Preoccupation with the problem of large size then leads naturally into a consideration of the common factors in big business and big government, with particular reference to the outside limits of administrative decentralization. There follows inevitably the question of what kind of a yardstick is available in appraising institutional performance — especially if the institution is large and noncompetitive — and hence the fourth essay deals with the concept of efficiency and its reliability as a basic tool for judging results. The last essay is entitled "Managerial Freedom and the Role of Government" and attempts to project some of the findings and conclusions into the future.

All of these are large and complicated subjects and the solutions to some of them are not known. It may appear foolhardy, therefore, to try to discuss them within the limits of a small volume. The justification is the author's desire to set forth a method of analysis and to suggest some tentative conclusions which may prove rewarding in the extensive and intensive cultivation of the borderland between business and government which all the signs indicate is going to take place.

A word of explanation as to why the term "administrative state" is used in the title. By this term, which has recently come into wide use, is meant the political state when it has taken on heavy responsibilities for operating the common affairs of the community, and especially those that deal with economic life. The administrative state is the civil

service state. It has been given so much to do that
administration threatens to overshadow policy-
making and politics. It is an interventionist state,
a state that owns and operates many diverse activities. With so much to do, management becomes the
dominant motif, and hence the appropriateness of
the term in the present title.

The free enterprise system, by comparison, may
be viewed as traditionally existing under conditions that are the antithesis of the administrative
state. To be compatible with the free enterprise
system, government must do varying amounts of
the right things and not too many of the wrong
things. The wrong things are administering too
much of the national economy and unwittingly
creating conditions, either by action or inaction,
which infringe on the freedom of management in-
digenous in the free enterprise system. On the
other hand, government has a necessary and positive
role relative to the economy if the system we call
free enterprise is to survive. What this line of
differentiation is and how it can successfully be
delineated through administration is one of the
main themes of the present essays.

On balance, however, the reader will find more
emphasis on common elements than on antitheses.
My thesis is that when concentration of power occurs it affects all institutions; that the bigger the
institutions of business and government become the
more they resemble each other; and that the way
to preserve the free enterprise system and popular

government is to decentralize—a procedure which, however, has its limitations. Individual ownership and numerous competing units are the conditions precedent of the free enterprise system. As we have drifted away from these conditions, we have steadily increased the possibility of the administrative state and of socialism.

This is not so much an attempt to write a political tract and an economic formula, however, as to understand what is happening to the institutions of business and government in terms of causal relationships and vital shifts of power within society.

I am grateful to the Southern Regional Training Program in Public Administration, and especially to its chairman, Dr. York Willbern, for the invitation to give the lecture series which forms the foundation of this volume. The lectures were given during the first week of November, 1950, at the University of Alabama, to the students and faculty of the Southern Regional Training Program, and in form the lectures remain virtually unchanged. I also wish to express gratitude to the Shinner Foundation of Chicago for the opportunity to spend a period of study in California in advance of giving these lectures. My wife, Gladys Ogden Dimock, assisted in the planning and execution of the task and to her I owe a deep debt of gratitude.

Scrivelsby   Marshall E. Dimock
Bethel, Vermont
December, 1950

CONTENTS

I

LIFE FACTORS OF FREE ENTERPRISE

THE FREE ENTERPRISE SYSTEM is said to be losing ground in the United States and to be giving way to an all-powerful "administrative state," which is the rule of the economy by government or by public administration.[1] That the first part of this statement is true seems to admit of little argument, for men of widely differing political persuasions apparently agree that free enterprise as we have known it is undergoing profound changes. That rule of the economy by public administration is what we are inescapably headed for, however, is certainly subject to several grains of doubt because, as will be pointed out, the collectivism which many see approaching is just as apt to be the private brand as it is the public brand.

I

If collectivism is a danger, then it is time to take stock of the situation. What is the free enterprise system, why is it worth saving, what is causing it to change, and why are private and public collectivism more alike than different? Actually, their

---

1. See, for example, Joseph Rosenfarb, *Freedom and the Administrative State* (New York, 1948), p. 75; or Dwight Waldo, *The Administrative State* (New York, 1948). The term "administrative state" is defined in the present author's preface.

distinguishing marks are institutionalism and management, frequently exhibiting characteristics of monopoly and great size.[2] It is with such questions that these explorations will be concerned, revolving as they do around a growing body of knowledge called administrative theory.

If the administrative state appears as a menace to the American way of life, it has come about in part, at least, because of a lack of understanding of what has been happening in the past few decades. Do we even know, for example, what it is we are trying to save? Stuart Chase in his book, *The Proper Study of Mankind,* chides the economists because their assumptions are incomplete, they neglect psychology and institutional behavior, and hence they are seldom able to describe reality or to predict what is actually going to happen. Chase is not sure whether free enterprise is anything that may be called a system, or that there are discoverable laws ruling its operation, but he does feel certain that if we are to solve large human relations problems, such as those growing out of the free enterprise system, there will have to be broader assumptions and more teamwork among the social scientists of the kind that made atomic energy possible in the physical sciences.[3]

2. That collectivism is a generic term and that its increase is due to cause-and-effect relationships, all resulting in the appearance of monopoly, in varying guises, is made clear by Henry Simons in *Economic Policy For a Free Society* (Chicago, 1948), especially pp. 4, 43.
3. Stuart Chase, *The Proper Study of Mankind: An Inquiry Into the Science of Human Relations* (New York, 1948), p. 213.

Apparently many businessmen feel much the same way about it. Not long ago, for example, a Chicago businessman made two points that struck home: first, that businessmen and economists do not seem to understand each other and hence there is a need to work out some common ground between them; and second, that businessmen are generally unrealistic and unreasonable in their attitudes toward government, to the extent of jeopardizing the future of the nation. He concluded with the remark that someone, preferably a business executive, should undertake to interpret the free enterprise system to the public, adding that only an executive could do the job because of the necessity of combining realism with theory.[4] This general attitude was officially expressed by the Economic Principles Commission of the National Association of Manufacturers, which in 1946 pointed out that "while there was much talk of the 'free enterprise system,' there was little real economic understanding of it and much need for its understanding; that there were many pamphlets about 'free enterprise,' but no serious books of definition and explanation."[5]

This, then, is the challenge: assuming that the free enterprise system is in fact being weakened,

---

4. Ernest G. Shinner, to the author in private conversation.
5. Economic Principles Commission, National Association of Manufacturers, *The American Individual Enterprise System: Its Nature, Evolution, and Future* (1946), in the foreword. It was explained that this two-volume study was undertaken in order to fill the need referred to in the quoted paragraph.

can we learn enough about what it is and how it
works, can we draw enough information from disciplines not heretofore called upon, can we reexam-
ine the whole area of administrative theory, and can
we do all this sufficiently quickly and thoroughly
to prevent any further undermining of the system
and restore it to vigor?

(By the free enterprise system I mean one in which
the predominant characteristics are individual ownership, competition, and managerial freedom —
these three, essentially, for other characteristics
which might be mentioned may be subsumed under
them.) The National Association of Manufacturers
prefers the term individual enterprise system to free
enterprise system because it seems to them a more
accurate description. The system, they say, is
"mainly competitive, on a private profit-or-loss
basis, and free within limits of laws enacted by representative government."[6] My definition does not
differ materially from theirs except that I am inclined to emphasize freedom of management more
than the essentially negative factor of freedom from
undue governmental restraint. This can be an important matter of difference, however, as will become clear.

By the term life factors I mean those total influ-
ences in nature and society which tend to maintain
the strength or sap the vitality of the system. Some
of these factors are hereditary but most of them
are environmental, some are nonhuman but most

6. *Ibid.*

of them are human, some are institutional and some are psychological, but all are broadly societal and involve both the economy and the government. In short, they are cause-and-effect relationships involving social pressures, tensions, and adjustments.

In speaking of the free enterprise system, therefore, I definitely do not mean a separate organism having an independent life of its own, in the manner the biologist considers life. The free enterprise system is simply a designation given to a particular form of group behavior in which institutional organization and functioning, psychological motivation and reward, and the relationships between private and public interest bear certain distinguishing characteristics. As in the physical realm, we may assume that most differences are in degree and in combination, and are not essential differences in substance and energy.

My thesis is that free enterprise consists of such things as individual ownership, rigorous competition, and freedom of management, all of which are easier to maintain in vigor when the culture is simple and uncomplicated than when it is complex and institutionalized. The problem, therefore, is to maintain the human factor in the artificial frame. How does one do this? By understanding the principles applicable to institutions, the relations between them, and the motivations which provide satisfactions and avoid destructive tensions. In achieving this end the disciplines of biology, anthropology, and social psychology must be called on in addition to economics, political science, and public administration.

I shall argue that it is the complexity of our culture—based as it is on advanced technology and large aggregations of power—that causes most of the difficulties of our free enterprise system, that decentralization of industry is not the whole answer, that claims of superior efficiency through large size are not entirely justified, that security can best be assured through an understanding of the proper role of government, and that in this manner the threat of the administrative state can be neutralized.

Since the situation is complex, the analysis, if it is to be complete and realistic, seems to require the joint efforts of researchers from more than one discipline. The basic principle involved here was stated by Munro in 1928: "No branch of knowledge advances by itself. In its progress it draws others along."[7] When physics and chemistry move forward, for example, the task is set for economics and political science. "Ever fed by the irrepressible curiosity of the scientist and inventor," said Charles A. Beard, "technology marches in seven-league boots, from one ruthless, revolutionary conquest to another. . . ."[8] Stuart Chase also, I think, has

7. William Bennett Munro, "Physics and Politics—An Old Analogy Revised," *American Political Science Review*, Vol. 22 (Feb. 1928), p. 2.
8. Charles A. Beard, "Time, Technology, and the Creative Spirit in Political Science," *American Political Science Review*, Vol. 21 (Feb. 1927), p. 5.

shown pretty conclusively that the toughest problems of social science—such as the causes and cures of war and the reconciliation of security and freedom—can be resolved only through a coöperative approach on the part of the social sciences in which the culture concept (the broadest possible view of man's interrelations in society) is taken as the point of departure and scientific method is the tool of analysis and synthesis.[9]

Perhaps some comfort may be had from Buckle's generalization to the effect that the deepest truths of any science are found not at its center but on its periphery where it impinges on all the other sciences. The present problem involves an overlapping of many peripheries. An understanding of the free enterprise system and what must be done to maintain it requires more than a knowledge of formal economics or even of economics and political science; it seems necessary also to draw from sociology and social psychology. In fact, if we would be scientifically fortified, we must draw from anthropology as well—that bridgehead between the physical and the social sciences—because from its researches are secured data which are indispensable. Kroeber, for example, one of the greatest of his profession, points out that "On the basis of probability . . . , some cultures are likely to have changed at some time from one class to another. This in turn indicates that sets toward co-operation, competition, and individualism are not necessarily

9. Chase, *op. cit.*, Ch. 6.

among the more permanent trends of development; and this suggests that they are secondary rather than deep-seated characteristics."[10] He adds that our own society has "undergone considerable shift from a competitive-individualistic to a co-operative orientation in the last forty years, without fully equivalent change in the basic content of its culture." The question is, Why? Because if we could clearly isolate the reasons we might then, possibly for the first time, be in a position to exercise a controlling influence on shifts of direction so far as free enterprise is concerned. If the verdict of anthropology is correct, we should be able to retrace our steps toward private ownership and individualism even after we had gone some distance on the way to monopoly and collectivism.

II

If problems connected with growth are the key to the vitality and survival of the free enterprise system, we must turn first to biology and anthropology for clues as to what is involved, and then to a careful examination of technological causation, the principal factor inducing change.

Many writers on the free enterprise system, either consciously or unconsciously, show the influence of the biological analogy. It is an old tradition going all the way back to Plato and Aristotle and

10. A. L. Kroeber, *Anthropology: Race, Language, Culture, Psychology, Prehistory* (New York, rev. ed., 1948), p. 595.

more recently has affected all of the social sciences, especially sociology and political science.[11] However, it was in the writings of Herbert Spencer (1820-1903), influenced by Darwin, that the organismic theory first received systematic development and made its powerful impact on later social analysis. The original theories have been considerably modified by later sociologists and anthropologists but there are still insights and even principles which help to explain why the free enterprise system is experiencing the pains which usually accompany growth and change.

In enumerating his six fundamental similarities between society and a physical organism, Spencer mentions two factors that appear especially important to the present inquiry: first, that as either society or a physical organism increases in size, it inceases also in complexity of structure; and second, that progressive differentiation of structure in each case is accompanied by a like differentiation of function (i.e., division of labor.)[12] Following Darwin's lead, Spencer was best known, of course, for his advocacy of social evolution, for he saw society progressing steadily from a militaristic and warlike existence to one of peaceful industrialism. This last goal, however, could not be attained until society had been equilibrated with the physical environ-

---

11. Dealt with in H. E. Barnes (ed.), *An Introduction to the History of Sociology* (Chicago, 1948), pp. 115-116, 210-211, 459.
12. Herbert Spencer, *Principles of Sociology* (New York, 1896), Vol. I, Pts. I and II.

ment, groups with the state, and nations and races with each other.[13]

The most significant aspect of the biological analogy, however, is not as it relates to structure or function, but in its emphasis on adaptations to environment. Change and adjustment must be assumed to be unending, and the problem is to retain the values of any system, such as individualism, private ownership of property, and freedom—all of which Spencer highly prized—while at the same time adapting to the inexorable demands of organic, functional, and environmental change.

Now there are many things wrong with the biological analogy. The first is that any subject should develop its own data and principles, not by analogy—which is precarious—but by rigorous application of the scientific method. Analogy may lead to half-truths possessing a fatal fascination but causing bad mistakes in thinking and policy. Social theorists have sometimes fallen into the trap of speaking of society in terms of the problem of age incident to various periods in the life of the individual. How often it is said, for example, that the American system is "mature;" that rugged individualism disappeared with the frontier; that in our old age we must be cautious and coöperative; that as one projects the trends of recent years, it will be seen that socialism is inevitable; or conversely, that the system has inherent power; that it is a distinc-

13. See Giddings' summary of Spencer's views in *Sociology: A Lecture* (New York, 1908), pp. 29-30.

tive organism; that new frontiers are constantly opening; that we are not yet mature and most of life lies ahead. It is also superficially argued that since evolution is predestined, and organisms proceed from lower to higher forms of life, man's social existence must be expected to follow this same course of steady progression irrespective of how many mistakes society makes or the degree to which a people may direct their destinies.

This viewpoint has long been discarded in the biological. sciences and it is now almost dead in social science analysis as well. Kroeber points out that two or three generations ago, under the spell of the theory of evolution in its first flush, a complacent view of progress was perhaps to be expected, but today such views are threadbare and reserved for "newspaper science or have become a matter for idle amateur guessing."[14] He does record a scientifically demonstrable conclusion, however, when he says that "in an over-all sort of way, the sum total of culture of mankind has pretty continuously grown in bulk through history, and that recessions in civilization either are local and likely to be compensated for elsewhere; or they primarily affect patterns of organization and the values of their products — cultural qualities."[15] This last proviso is an important one, of course, because it includes the free enterprise system itself, since it is so largely a matter of organization and values.

14. Kroeber, *op. cit.,* pp. 6-7.
15. *Ibid.,* p. 297.

If, as Kroeber suggests, progress is not automatic and trends are in fact changeable, then some important inferences emerge: Progress must be sustained by a knowledge of human relations as well as by a knowledge of technology; Marx, following Hegel's philosophy of history, was wrong in assuming that capitalism would inevitably break down in consequence of its own internal weaknesses; and those sociologists who predict the future by projecting current trends are not necessarily correct in assuming that the political economy of the United States will evolve into socialism. The future depends, rather, on how much we learn about cause-and-effect relationships and institutional operation, and whether we apply what we learn in time to reverse trends which are now clearly under way.

Collecting the threads of the discussion to this point, it seems safe to say that change is constant but that progress is not; that growth leads to complexity and specialization, which increase the number of problems for society; that in complicated social mechanisms there are greater chances of malfunctioning because there are more parts to be meshed and more stresses and strains that may develop; and that hence the more complex the organism becomes the greater the degree of intelligence that must be applied if society is to survive and prosper. Kroeber points out that "Culture is the special and exclusive product of men, and is their distinctive quality in the cosmos." And what is culture? It is the mass of learned and transmitted motor reactions, habits, techniques, ideas, and values—and the behavior they induce.[16] I wish he had added organization and institutions to his list because the more intricate a culture becomes the more imporatnt these prove to be.

It is out of this complex of factors that we must find the key to the successful operation of the free enterprise system. Main reliance must be on man's cognitive powers, his distinctive ability to choose the values and the appropriate institutions with which to fulfil his needs and aspirations. When, therefore, any school of economic analysis assumes that nature, not man, is a sufficient regulator of complex social and economic life, we are, by the fact of such oversimplification, storing up trouble for ourselves in the form of future inevitable disequilibriums. Although clearly we should make every effort to live in accord with nature's laws, it is a mistake to assume that nature will do our thinking and our contriving for us.

In the light of these considerations I am prepared for the broadening and revising of fundamental economic analysis that has been taking place in recent years. The main outlines of such a revision were suggested by Gardiner C. Means in an article appearing in 1935.[17] Classical economics as-

16. *Ibid.*, p. 8.
17. Gardiner C. Means, "The Distribution of Control and Responsibility in a Modern Economy," *Political Science Quarterly*, Vol. 50 (Mar. 1935), pp. 59-69; reprinted, with revisions, in B. E. Lippincott (ed.) *Government Control of the Economic Order* (Minneapolis, 1935), pp. 1-17.

sumes that the non-human forces of the market are an automatic and reliable regulator and that human intelligence and contriving are unnecessary and even objectionable. But actual experience has increasingly shown that administrative organization and human decision-making play a growing part in the actual conduct of affairs both by individual business firms and by governmental policy decision. Hence when traditional economists underrate the role of social associations and administrative organizations, they cannot expect to provide a realistic analysis of what is actually happening. Gradually but steadily, great segments in the organization of economic activity have shifted from the market place to administration and with the development of the huge semi-public corporation, in which ownership is divorced from control, even the character of private property has changed in those areas of the economy.

Problems of organization, management, power relationships, and control have been the traditional focus of attention of social science disciplines other than economics, and especially of political science. As early as 1927 Charles A. Beard was of the opinion that "Particularly can we fertilize political science by a closer affiliation with the economists, who now seem to have cast off their Manchester dogmas and laid their minds alongside the changing processes of production and distribution."[18] But in 1935 Means, the economist, was saying to his brethren in

18. Beard, *op. cit.,* p. 11.

adjoining disciplines, "It is in the development of further administrative coordination that we must come to political scientists for aid. We ask that you apply to the field of economic administration the technique of analysis and principles of organization which you have developed in the study of the state."[19] This underscores the view, previously expressed, that the preservation of the free enterprise system seems to require the joint analysis of more than one social science discipline if the resulting formulation is to be complete and realistic.

Now it may be objected, as it has been by classical economists such as Hayek, that mankind would be better off if we had deliberately allowed ourselves to be regulated solely by the impersonal forces of the market, avoiding the man-made decisions of large corporations, trade unions, farmers' organizations, and legislatures. Theoretically this is supportable. The difficulty is that such an approach emphasizes preference, or what *should* be, and so fails to describe what *is* the actual course of social and economic behavior. In this case we must choose between preference and science and the wiser counsel seems to be to pin our faith on science, while doing everything possible to change conditions materially enough to allow our preferences to operate in the way we should like to see them operate.

American social science has characteristically emphasized the volitional in contrast to the automatic, human determinations instead of those which

19. Means, *op. cit.*, p. 8.

nature, unaided, is supposed to make. Thus Lester Ward (1841-1913), the first systematic sociologist produced in the United States, argued that energy must be controlled if evolution is to come about. As between the unconscious control of nature and the conscious direction of mind, the latter, thought Ward, is manifestly superior. Nature is wasteful in providing an immense mass of raw materials and leaving them to be improved slowly through natural selection.[20] The tendency of human intelligence is to economize through foresight and the adjustment of means to ends. Further, control of the dynamic forces of nature and society through the adjustment of means to ends is what Ward designated as telesis, a term derived from his background as a botanist.

This is not to suggest that mind alone (i.e., rationality) rules human conduct, but merely to make clear that neutral nature, unassisted, is an insufficient regulator of social behavior. As MacIver points out, all group activity consists of myths (belief systems) and techniques (methods), both of which play important and interacting roles in the governance of the economy, the social fabric, and the political state.[21] The free enterprise system itself, therefore, is a combination of these two elements, belief system and technique. As myths change, society turns its techniques to different uses; and as techniques advance, man's myths re-

20. Lester Ward, *Pure Sociology* (New York, 1903), pp. 463 ff.
21. R. M. MacIver, *The Web of Government* (New York, 1947), pp. 1-6.

sponsively take a new range. To this basic analysis Leighton has added other principles of social dynamics, namely, that human groups cannot effectively carry out acts for which they have no underlying systems of belief; and that when, through failure to adjust to tension caused by technology and other factors of change, the community under stress becomes more emotional, unstable, and conflicting, it is less able to deal with its problems.[22] It would appear, therefore, that the future health of the free enterprise system depends in part at least, on two factors: a recognition of what causes change and tensions to appear, and secondly, the avoidance of an undue emotionalism which only serves to handicap the system's defenders.

III

Although the biological analogy is unquestionably useful in helping to explain social and economic change, an understanding of the effects of technology is even more useful and essential to the skillful guidance of the free enterprise system. Munro observes that "Every new application of science makes life more complex and hence government [presumably, also, social science] more complex; for the difficulties . . . increase as the square of newly-created human problems."[23] This point of view has long been adopted in anthropol-

22. Alexander H. Leighton, *The Governing of Men* (Princeton, 1945), pp. 292, 302.
23. Munro, *op. cit.*, p. 8.

ogy, sociology, and political science, and now is increasingly taken as a point of departure by those who seek a more realistic analysis of economics.

Life in a simple culture creates no great social problem, as a rule, because private ownership, a minimum of pressure group activity, and governmental functions kept within proper bounds are inherent in the situation. I must confess, for example, that I did not fully appreciate some of the finer values of the free enterprise system, even intellectually, and surely not to the greatest extent emotionally, until I went to live in the state of Vermont. There I find that most people own their own family-sized farms or small businesses and respect private property because it is secured by the sweat of their brows and their own initiative and independence; because of a strong sense of individual, family, and community responsibility, few need public assistance and few have more worldly possessions than the average; there is a deep suspicion of too much power concentrated anywhere in society—in business, government, or labor; and running throughout is a blend of rugged individualism combined with social coöperation, a general willingness to share the responsibilities of government and office-holding combined with a universal vigilance lest government do things that could just as well or better be done by the citizens themselves, individually or in groups.

To experience free enterprise at its best, as it is in the Vermont environment, not only produces

deep emotional satisfactions but also creates a desire to study the reasons that economic freedom and
democracy are seemingly so much harder to maintain in a complex social environment like that of
most of the rest of the nation where communities
are generally more dependent on large technological installations and their products.

In pointing to the problems of adjustment created by physical and social invention, however, the
impression must not be conveyed that technology
is for that reason an evil and subversive factor, even
threatening, as some believe, the very existence of
free enterprise and popular government. This point
of view has sometimes been expressed even by
scientists, especially since the conversion of atomic
energy into the materials of destruction. In the
long haul, most people would probably agree with
Morgan, the sociologist, whose basic theory of society was technological. Culture, he said, advances
as the technological means of man's control over
his habitat, particularly over the means of subsistence, are enlarged and improved; ". . . the great
epochs of human progress have been identified,
more or less directly, with the enlargement of the
sources of subsistence."[24] Or take the recent statement of Morris L. Cooke, the engineer and management consultant: one may almost say that technology creates resources, "for what is coal if man
has no means other than his hands to take it from
the earth, or water power if he cannot harness it;

24. Lewis Henry Morgan, *Ancient Society* (New York, 1877), p. 19.

what are acres of grain if they cannot be harvested in season, converted into food, and carried to those who need it?" Nor is the end of technological advance in sight, says this engineer: "It is the lever by which men can lift themselves to higher standards of living and thus, by transcending physical urgencies——goods, clothing, shelter——enhance the dignity and freedom of the individual."[25] This is the potentiality; but between potentiality and accomplishment there is, in social dynamics, a broad gulf that must be spanned by social knowledge and technique.

Technology *might* be the cause of undermining our free institutions if we were to fail soon enough to discover as much about social laws as we know about physical laws. Increasingly physical scientists as well as social scientists agree with Munro's dictum that, "to be safe, our progress in the art of government [and social life generally] ought to be faster than the advance of applied science."[26] What is needed, therefore, is an analysis of cause-and-effect relationships beginning with invention and proceeding logically to ultimate consumer satisfactions brought about through the institutions and motivations of society. Barnes, following Morgan's analysis, holds that a simple, sound theory of cultural evolution proceeds in this way: "Man lives by exploiting the resources of nature by technological

25. Morris L. Cooke, "Resources," in S. E. Harris (ed.) *Saving American Capitalism* (New York, 1948), pp. 109-110.
26. Munro, *op. cit.*, p. 9.

means. Social institutions are society's ways of organizing itself to wield and use its technology. As the technology advances, social institutions must change also."[27]

But this leaves unanswered the question of why change is inevitable. Many illustrations might be afforded but I take one that recently I was allowed to read about in an address prepared by a prominent businessman who speaks under the auspices of the National Association of Manufacturers.[28] The inventions of the laboratory have led to the production of labor-saving devices in industry. In the Middle Ages, laborers owned their own tools and hence derived status and satisfactions as members of society. With invention, however, they typically own no tools of their own but merely operate machines owned by others. With the invention of the modern corporation, there may be thousands of stockholders served by paid managerial executives. One of the problems which results is how to give to laborers the status and vocational satisfactions they derived when they owned their own tools. Labor unions develop powerful associations in order to attain bargaining equality with management, causing the organized political state to interfere. Management is placed in a position where more is expected in terms of leadership ability and qualities than sometimes seems humanly possible. With

27. Barnes, *op. cit.*, p. 141.
28. N. Henry Gellert, President, Seattle Gas Company, Seattle, Washington.

thousands of stockholders, the functions of ownership are changed because power has been transferred from owners to paid managers. Hence,
through a direct cause-and-effect cycle, invention
produces big machines, large corporations, powerful
labor unions, big government, and delicate balances
between private and public institutions.

The question, therefore, is whether our social
and managerial skills can keep pace with technology
in order that the system of private ownership, competition, and free management which has made this
nation great may continue on its steady course. The
businessman who has just been referred to, like
most, is suspicious of social theorists and prefers to
follow an empirical entity called "social skills," but
when this total analysis is laid alongside that of most
social science analyses, there is not much of difference that stands out except, perhaps, minor ones of
vocabulary. If those who wield power as policy-
makers and managers in industry, agriculture, labor,
and government were to think as consecutively
about the problems of the free enterprise system as
this businessman, there is reason to believe that
Munro's plea for the development of a social science
in advance of rather than lagging behind the technology which creates many of its major problems,
might rapidly take shape.

The central problem created by technology is
the power, the concentration of authority, which
inevitably accompanies bigness and complexity. In
a simple culture like that of Vermont, the problem

is a minor one but in the United States Steel Corporation, the Congress of Industrial Organizations, or the federal government, the question of power is of primary concern. A series of questions centers around the concept of power: How big must a corporation be in order to make the best use of technology? How much concentration of power may be vested in a few corporations without threatening to destroy competition in whole areas of the economy? When corporations become large enough —through individual growth or action in concert with others—to determine how resources shall be allocated and what prices shall prevail, does the resulting creation of administered price areas cause a breakdown of naturally-induced prices in other parts of the economy? How big and powerful may labor unions become before they begin to encroach on the authority traditionally exercised by managers and owners under the private-profit system? And what of government? Harassed by pressure groups seeking favors for themselves and regulation of the other fellow, government may eventually become larger and more powerful than any segment of the economy standing alone. Problems of regulation and assistance, welfare and conservation, extend the already swollen confines of government. Soon the question arises, how big may government become and how many economic and welfare functions may it perform without undermining the freedom and self-reliance which are essential ingredients of the free enterprise system?

Now to be sure, these problems are not always as serious as they sometimes appear because developments which occur rapidly always magnify themselves more than if they occurred over a longer period of time. But the fact remains that today they are rapid enough and startling enough to cause widespread insecurity and fear, which is why irrational emotion instead of sober calculation is still all too common a phenomenon. Big business fears strong labor and government, labor fears big business and government, agriculture fears big business, big labor, and big government, too, except when the farmers feel sure of governmental support.[29] The only factor common to all groups seems to be that at one time or another each of the Big Three of industry, labor, and agriculture feels strongly about and against big government. Being emotional about the matter, such pressure groups refuse to admit their part in calling big government into existence and hence salve their damaged feelings by calling the government "they," although in a democracy "they" is always "we." Instead of assuming its proportionate share of the responsibility for producing big government, each group seeks a scapegoat or a devil, the very fact of which militates against the likelihood that it will readily find the true cause-and-effect relationship and take effective steps to reverse existing trends.

Alexander Leighton has done a valuable service

29. Spelled out in Stuart Chase, *Democracy Under Pressure* (New York, 1945).

of social psychology analysis in dissecting the behavior pattern of individuals and groups under stress. His enunciation of priciples under the heading, "The Way People React to Stress," should be required reading for all who claim to be attached to the preservation of the free enterprise system. He points out, for example, that one result of submission to authority may be to lead the individual to extremes of blind submission that rob him of the ability to take care of himself; that one result of withdrawal may be to lead to extremes of selfishness, isolation, personal deterioration, and unreliability; that a consequence of aggression may be "confused and violent action wholly inappropriate to the circumstances . . . "; that aggression combined with fear may lead to attacks on persons having little or nothing to do with the causes of stress; and that "following an outburst of aggressive action, there is usually a period in which the individual has a sense of relief and well-being."[30] Anyone with a sense of humor and a New England conscience can doubtless recognize himself in some of these characteristics.

An aspect of the concept of power is the question of motive. How can incentives be preserved, and in some cases stimulated, but finally checked before they lead to too great accumulations of power? The success of any system depends on effective motivation and reward and it is in this area that some of the largest untapped reserves of motive power are

30. Leighton, *op. cit.*, pp. 264-274.

found. In the past, motivation was considered self-generating, but that was in a more simple culture characterized by relatively few tensions and frustrations. Profit-making has always been the strongest force flowing through the free enterprise system and it is still the main goad to efficiency and accomplishment. But it must be remembered that the concept of profit is vastly different in an institutional civilization, involving coöperation and teamwork, than it was in one dependent on robber barons and individualists.

Motivation has become a complicated business in large institutions. Mayo, Kornhauser, and others have found that factors such as status, security, prestige, and recognition for loyal service are powerful incentives and that at times they may even rival or surpass the strictly remunerative reward. This does not mean that the profit motive might be deposed; it merely means that motivation in large institutions is complex and that if our psychologists, personnel people, and executives can uncover some of the deeper truths in this area they might provide additional tools for strengthening and maintaining a system of individual ownership, operation, and reward. It is also possible that a better balance of incentives might lead to a better balance of power. Someone has recently said that the chain reactions of human relations are more important than those of atoms. Those close to big institutions, with their frustrations and stupendous energies, might be inclined to agree.

The next task is to analyze the concept of power as applied to modern large-scale social organizations. Here one turns with profit to MacIver's book, *The Web of Government*. Power, he says is universally found in all large organization, whether it be government, the modern corporation, the trade union, the Roman Catholic Church, or the agencies of information and propaganda. Social power is the capacity to control the behavior of others either directly by fiat or indirectly by the manipulation of available means. "The power of government," he continues, "is one aspect of power among many. It is formally supreme, in the sense that government alone has the ultimate right to use direct coercion. Formally it assigns limit and place to all other exercisers of power. But this statement is barren if not supplemented by the further statement that government itself is a creature of society and is subject to the pulls and pressures of the other foci of power. What power the government wields and to what ends it directs this power depends on these other forces, on the manner in which they are operatively adjusted to one another in the struggle and clash, the convergence and divergence, of power-possessing interests."[31]

There are some findings of MacIver's which, though true, many will not like to admit. For example, in modern American industry, as we have already remarked, power attaches far more to the management than to the ownership of property,

31. MacIver, *op. cit.*, pp. 87-91.

and this fact "tends to create a certain resemblance between the power structure of capitalism and that of socialism."[32] Or again: "The leader of a great trade union organization can now, under favorable conditions, dictate to president or king, and may finally elevate himself to the highest position in the land."[33] Nor will the leaders of pressure groups like to be told that "the authority of government does not create the order over which it presides and does not sustain that order solely by its own fiat or its accredited power. There is authority beyond the authority of government. There is a greater con-census without which the fundamental order of the community would fall apart."[34] If government tends to become so big and powerful as to under-mine the free enterprise system, the pressure groups which control government should point an accus-ing finger at themselves and not at a nebulous "they."

Now there is a certain amount of truth in the "creeping paralysis" theory which Hayek, Flynn,[35] and others have made popular. MacIver states it in the form of a universal principle applicable to all institutions, and as such it offers a much more re-liable guide than when directed to only one insti-tution: "Power of any kind seeks its own increase." The owners of power strive to extend and solidify

32. *Ibid.*, p. 88.
33. *Ibid.*, p. 88.
34. *Ibid.*, p. 85.
35. Friedrich A. Hayek, *The Road to Serfdom* (Chicago, 1944); John T. Flynn, *The Road Ahead* (New York, 1949).

their dominance. But, in government as elsewhere, they are human beings like the rest, have other goals as well, and are not at one concerning these other goals.[36] It is just as foolish to dream up a conspiracy of Washington officials, on the assumption that they spend their nights devising ways to undermine the free enterprise system, as it used to be when farmers believed that all of Wall Street was engaged in a close conspiracy against the rest of the nation. To the extent that "Washington," "the government," "bureaucracy," and similar epithets constitute the currency of attacks by free enterprise on the problems which beset it, to that extent, I fear, those who are chiefly responsible for sound and energetic counsel are self-defeating, for they center their fire on the result, not the cause. Instead of patiently setting forth all the contributing factors in a complex situation, they tend to lump them all into one, and a minor one at that, compared with technology or the rapidity of social change.

IV

(A study of the problem of change shows that invention, like growth, causes social complexity. Certain results of complexity stand out: there is more need for the intricate mechanisms of coöperation and less opportunity for individualistic pioneering; man-made decisions become increasingly important as natural forces are superseded; power

36. MacIver, *op. cit.*, p. 92.

accumulates in institutions and in the top management officials responsible for policy and decision; rules and regulations become imperative, replacing the intuitive judgment of individual enterprisers; pressure groups cause government increasingly to interfere in all areas of social and economic life, setting up an unending cycle of aggression and defense; and the effect of institutional life generally is to restrict the freedom of the individual and to weaken the satisfactions which he experiences when running alone. From this it seems clear that because of the complex social and economic situation in which we find ourselves today, we must acquire a better understanding of the life factors which maintain the vitality of the free enterprise system if we would overcome the institutional difficulties which act as a depressant to enterprise and individual freedom. I feel confident that this is possible.

The first principle to catch hold of is that excessive power, in any form, is dangerous and that hence the degree of power accumulating in any one place should be held to an irreducible minimum. Too much power in large corporations is as objectionable as too much power in government officials. The principle is exactly the same. Power leads to envy, envy to insecurity, insecurity to radical measures of reform. Insecurity and fear are the besetting dangers of our day, in all classes of the population, and the reason seems to be that we have less control over our individual destinies than formerly and are swept along by collective forces. Moreover, these collective forces are at least as much due to developments within industry, labor, and agriculture as they are to corresponding developments in the field of government. Indeed, private collectivism can be more dangerous in its social effects and uses than public collectivism, because the latter is usually more responsible and more closely checked than the former.

It is hard to convince the wielders of power that too much power is a bad thing, as our Revolutionary ancestors once learned and as we have since forgotten. But if our leaders cannot be convinced of this truth, then there seems little chance of effective and permanent reform. Capitalism and the democratic state need a self-denying ordinance limiting excessive power. Excessive outside compulsion is not only objectionable, but alone, it can never do the job.

With power there goes an accompanying responsibility, what the French call *noblesse oblige*. We have not been as quick to learn this lesson, perhaps, as our size and position in the world would seem to indicate, for our technology inevitably requires that large amounts of power must be administered in business and in government even under ideal conditions of voluntary self-restraint. That we are making some progress, however, is illustrated in an interesting address on "The Corporation's Responsibility to the Future," given by the president of the Standard Oil Company of New Jersey. Mr.

Holman states his belief that the corporation has a responsibility to continue as a creative force in society, to study and to promote better human relations with employees, stockholders, and the public, and to study the present-day economic situations of which it is both a cause and an effect, coöperating in this task with others and making economic truth as widely known as possible.[37]

The second principle, a corollary of the first, is that power must be widely distributed if free enterprise and popular government are to endure. Each should get what he is entitled to and none should get too much. Corporations should be numerous and competitive, not few and large. Given this set of conditions, then labor unions should organize and operate on a unit-of-management rather than on a nation-wide basis. Every function that can be taken from the federal government and satisfactorily administered (an important proviso!) at the state or local level should be transferred as rapidly as possible. But here again, the wielders of power must want to do these things or there is little likelihood of far-reaching effects.

How can decentralization be accomplished? The question is discussed in Chapter III of this book but a few comments here are appropriate. Once there is a favorable climate of opinion toward this objective, decentralization should be accomplished by voluntary action as well as through the general

37. Eugene Holman, in an address given at Rensselaer Polytechnic Institute, October 14, 1949.

instrumentality of the antitrust laws and the encouragement of independent business, especially new businesses. Success, however, depends on the move being made simultaneously and synchronously by the Big Three and by government because no group can be expected to give ground unless the others are willing to go along.

The first of the three ingredients of the free enterprise system, the private ownership of property, is its greatest strength. When people own property—and especially if it is their means of livelihood—then they feel secure. As things stand today, there is a widespread feeling of insecurity that causes people to turn to government for ever new controls and remedies. To strengthen the free enterprise system, therefore, there must be more ownership and more operators of their own businesses —whether that business be commerce, farming, or skilled labor. Capitalism is shared ownership, but true sharing is not through the large corporation or the benevolent state; it is through personal ownership of the means of livelihood. Ownership of stock certificates is not the same thing. Our national policy as a people should therefore be directed toward a large number of smaller businesses, owner-operated, and away from giant corporations in which private ownership loses its distinctive character. The so-called managerial society may or may not be a prelude to socialism but one thing is sure: it is as different from the individual ownership of one's own means of livelihood as the spectator in the stands is from the baseball player on the field.

Sumner, the sociologist, has pointed out that a people desiring slow and orderly change must emphasize two factors above others: clear-cut beliefs and the private possession of property.[38] Lately in our American culture we have been inclined to overlook both of these points, for we think first of profit-making and we underrate the importance of private ownership by stripping it of its managerial control functions.

[The case for competition, the second ingredient of free enterprise, is increasingly confused in the public mind because we tend to regard competition as the antithesis of coöperation. As an abstract ethical matter, of course, most people will vote a preference in favor of coöperation and against competition. But this is not the question involved. Competition is an essential concomitant of private ownership, for if there are many owners there will be many competitors for consumer favor. Each enterpriser will try his best to attract business and in that process his own efficiency and that of his competitors will tend to improve. Competition causes managers to be public-relations-minded and hence guards against complacency and red tape. In short, competition in the economy is a system of organization and a process of supplying wants, not an ethical antithesis to coöperation.] This is made clear by simply noting the fact that coöperation also is necessary·in the operation of any business—

38. See a summary of his position in Barnes, *op. cit.*, Ch. VI.

coöperation between sellers, buyers, and employees —if the enterprise is to show a financial profit.

Another cause of fuzziness here is public dissatisfaction with the excesses of competition — the so-called cutthroat type, which may be and usually is clearly unethical. But this is no excuse for confused thinking on the general merits of competition as a condition of individual ownership and diffused power. At the risk of being accused of dogmatism, it may be said that no one of the three ingredients of the free enterprise system—private property, competition, and managerial freedom—may be eliminated and the other two maintained. Business support for this middle ingredient seems to be more in peril than support for the others, for it is widely apparent that competition has lost ground in recent years. Here again, therefore, what dominant public opinion thinks about this matter is likely to be the ultimately controlling factor. The statement of principles of the National Association of Manufacturers previously referred to[39] is unequivocal in its insistence on competition as an essential aspect of free enterprise. Competitive freedom, says the NAM, assures choice of activities suitable to ability, stimulates the full use of capacities, keeps the economy fluid, prevents stratification of people into rigid classes, encourages the development of specialized skills, and spurs enterprise to satisfy people's wants. Monopoly, in contrast, tends to be wasteful and inefficient. If one

39. *The American Individual Enterprise System*, *op. cit.*, pp. 8-9.

fully believes this, therefore, one cannot logically oppose the efforts of government to check monopoly and to encourage conditions favorable to competition, for the continuance of the system depends on such positive action.[40] This being the case, the current argument that antitrust prosecutions of industrial giants is an attack on *all* business is seen as fallacious and insupportable and designed merely to appeal to the prejudices of other businessmen.

The third element of the free enterprise system is managerial freedom. Every individual in an institution works better and gets greater satisfaction from the relationship when free to work things out his own way rather than being forced to operate according to rote and under rigid supervision. Powerful psychological incentives are involved here—status, self-fulfilment, pride of craftsmanship. The researches of Elton Mayo and his associates show that these factors are as important as, or even more important than, monetary reward and profit-making, although these also are indispensable.[41] In the private collectivism of giant corporations and the public collectivism of socialism, managerial freedom is much more difficult to secure and retain than under conditions of numerous independent

40. "If the function of government is confined to the elimination of monopoly and the punishment of collusive efforts designed to restrict or destroy competition, and to certain underwriting functions, the creative power of private enterprise . . . can be preserved."— Harold G. Moulton, *The American Economy* (Los Angeles, 1949).
41. Elton Mayo, *The Social Problems of an Industrial Civilization* (Boston, 1945), and *The Human Problems of an Industrial Civilization* (New York, 1933).

firms in a competitive frame. Freedom to earn a
profit, accompanied by the equal freedom to sustain a loss, is another powerful stimulus to efficiency, and these freedoms also inhere in a system
characterized by individual ownership, competition,
and free management.

In listing ten factors that may tend to undermine
the free enterprise system, therefore, Sumner Slichter underscores "The decline in the spirit of enterprise and in the willingness of business managers
to take chances."[42] He quotes Thurman Arnold
with apparent approval to the effect that "The im-
pelling faith of today is that investments must be
secure." If the willingness to take risks were ever
seriously to atrophy, that alone might sound the
death-knell of the individual enterprise system.

In summary it may be repeated that the basic
ingredients of the free enterprise system are individual ownership, competition, and freedom of
management, that the system must not be allowed
to slow down as a result of reaching what some
call maturity, and that it must remain flexible and
not become rigid. Power must be widely shared
and not concentrated. Newcomers must be able to
break in, if they have the ability, and hence those
already in the field must not become so large or so
conspiratorial that they can effectively deny access.
New inventions and new techniques are essential to

42. Sumner Slichter, *The American Economy, Its Problems and Prospects* (New York, 1948), p. 164.

growth and expansion, but from them we may expect serious wrenches and adjustments causing social change. Relationships which were once highly personal in a small enterprise, now tend toward impersonality, with the result that today's leaders must learn more than formerly about human nature and motivation. Above all else, however, is needed a precise knowledge of the laws of social dynamics, why pressures applied to institutions and people cause certain adjustments requiring certain responses if tensions are to be avoided and the values of the system maintained.) Once we learn the basic principles and causes we shall not have to fall back on stubborn dogmatism and frenzied emotion. Our leaders need social skills even more than they need belief systems.

In all these developing interrelationships, none, perhaps, is more important than clear thinking about the proper role of government in the total context. Businessmen who "get mad" and strike out blindly when the name of government is mentioned perform a disservice to the cause of free enterprise by their very lack of discrimination. Whether we like it or not, society must have government and it is our government, not the hostage of a minority group or dictatorship. As our servant, government performs essential functions in the realms of international relations, defense, protection of persons and property, and community services which businessmen are bound to applaud and support. How foolish and short-sighted it is, then, to condemn government in toto for some interference in economic affairs that we think it should not touch.

The more reasonable course is to make government more responsible and to see that it is more ably led, both as to policy and administration. If this were done more often it is quite possible that government would undertake fewer functions and would concentrate on those that are essential. (It would concentrate on those *preventive* measures which contribute to the maintenance of competition and the free enterprise system, adopt measures to encourage risk-taking and strong incentive, and lay long-range plans to avoid periods of serious unemployment and stagnant industry.)

But these results can be secured only by the active participation of those most able to provide their counsel and service; they will never be secured by a policy of withdrawal or vituperation. For the plain truth seems to be that the more government is despised and reviled by businessmen, the more it is required to do and the worse it is likely to do it. They key to this seemingly contradictory situation is found in the remark of former OPA administrator Chester Bowles, "If we are unprepared to accept *enough* government, we will end up with *too much*. It may be paradoxical but it is true. If we are reluctant to grant our government enough power to meet its essential tasks, the unsolved tasks will overtake us, and in the ensuing crisis we will be obliged to go far beyond what would have been necessary in government control had we taken adequate steps sooner."[43]

Jeremy Bentham, a wise social scientist, was in accord with this view. The challenge to the intelligent conservative, he said, is to determine the agenda of the state, meaning the irreducible minimum of functions the state must perform in order to maintain a vital economy. The more free enterprise does to avoid tensions, the less will the state have to step in. The less business does, the more the state will be called on to fill in the lacunae. If businessmen do not themselves realize that concentrated power is dangerous, competition essential, and widely diffused ownership the basic gratification, then the voters and pressure groups will demand redress of their grievances from the government.

The greatest need of American economic leadership, therefore, is an understanding of the principles underlying social change and the elements of stability; because with more statesmanship in the economy, there would be less need for government. The situation today is different from what it was even seventy-five years ago, when the open frontier and all it symbolized underlay the vitality of American capitalism. Now these physical freedoms are bounded and the life factors of free enterprise lie, rather, in a widespread comprehension of the cause-and-effect relationships that produce social, economic, and eventually political change.

43. Harris (ed.), *op. cit.*, p. 3.

II

MONOPOLY AND MANAGEMENT

Business magazines have been saying editorially that the most fateful issue of the next few years is what average Americans will decide concerning the merits of bigness and concentration. The preceding discussion has pointed to somewhat the same conclusion. The monopoly issue is involved in almost every other major question of public policy, including the causes of depressions and how to avoid them, whether agriculture and labor, as well as industry, are becoming monopolistic, and the survival of the free enterprise system itself.[1]

The June, 1949 number of the *American Economic Review* contains a symposium on the antitrust laws. Dexter Keezer, editor of the symposium, states that his own interest in the question stems largely from a desire to "maintain a safe base for political democracy" and that his principal concern is with the element of size and power, both basic considerations in determining what kind of an economy is safe for a democracy.[2] Another contributor is of the opinion that "The difficulties of restoring a high degree of competition are almost wholly

1. See, for example, Vernon A. Mund, *Government and Business* (New York, 1950), or the present author's *Business and Government* (New York, 1949), both of which are concerned with this theme.
2. "The Antitrust Laws: A Symposium," *American Economic Review*, Vol. 39 (June, 1949), pp. 718-723.

political and not economic or legal. Antitrust laws can be enforced where there is sufficient *will* to enforce them. . . ."[3] But does a strong enough will exist today to make any degree of success seem likely? Ben Lewis, of Oberlin, says no.[4] Wendell Berge repeats what he has stated so often and so well, that if the trend toward concentration cannot be stopped it will eventually mean the end of both our economic and political systems as we have known them in the past.[5] The American citizen, therefore, should ask himself whether concentration and bigness are good, bad, or of no consequence; whether these trends should be stopped, if possible; and if so, how it can best be done.

The answer to these questions is to be found largely in administrative theory. Although we do not as yet know enough about the problem of concentration to answer all elements of them with certainty and precision, there are no factors that cannot be clarified if social scientists are sufficiently skillful in analyzing the points at which more intensive research is needed.

I

What are the basic facts from which to take a reckoning? Sixty years ago the first of the antitrust laws was enacted to protect the free enterprise system from the corroding effects of monopoly in in-

3. Harlan L. McCracken, *ibid.*, p. 716.
4. *Ibid.*, p. 714.
5. *Ibid.*, p. 691.

dustry. Today, after more than half a century of trial, there is pretty general agreement that monopoly is more common and concentrations of economic power more prevalent than at any time in history, and that the trend is gaining momentum. Recent antitrust proceedings including the A & P and the Dupont cases, full-page advertisements in the newspapers urging readers to retain their faith in big business, and current discussions of the possibility of bringing organized labor under the antitrust laws point to a stubborn worrying over a problem which resists solution. It is true that of the seven or eight industrial giants against whom the Sherman Antitrust Act was aimed in 1890, only two remain in the same form today, but it is also true that America's 250 largest nonfinancial corporations control two thirds of the total industrial wealth of the country. And where in 1890 a million dollar corporation was a colossus, today bigness is measured not in millions but in billions of dollars' worth of assets.

The over-all trend toward bigness and monopoly began after the Civil War and has continued ever since, despite the antitrust laws. Recently the Department of Justice and the Federal Trade Commission have won some spectacular court cases, as in the decision outlawing uniform prices established through the basing point system, the decision prohibiting motion picture producers from monopolizing distribution, and other decisions for the first time making it plain that size, per se, may constitute so great a potential and actual threat to competition and the free market that bigness may of itself be objectionable. Appropriations for antitrust enforcement have been increased far and away over what they were in the 1920's or even the 1930's.[6]

But despite these encouraging signs, concentration seems to stride forward like a Paul Bunyon. New fields, once thought impervious to penetration by the giant chains, are constantly being invaded. The food industry is one. Manufacturing is another. Secretary of Commerce Sawyer recently published a list showing that with minor exceptions such as parts of the clothing industry and the service trades, the typical pattern of control in every area of the economy is through domination of the field by three or four big corporations.[7] Instead of being scattered among thousands of small competitors, competition is increasingly centered around the top few, which, at will, may agree not to reduce prices. There results a condition which makes economists despair of preserving our free enterprise system.

Some of the most significant and reliable facts are found in a Federal Trade Commission publication entitled *The Merger Movement*.[8] Here it is shown that merger—horizontal, vertical, and con-

6. Summarized in Dimock, *Business and Government* (New York, 1949), Chaps. 14-16.
7. Letter, with supporting data, addressed to the Hon. Emanuel Celler, chairman, Subcommittee on Study of Monopoly Power, Committee on the Judiciary, House of Representatives, Dec. 1, 1949.
8. Government Printing Office, 1948.

glomerate—has been the method most frequently used to effect a concentration. Because of the failure of Congress to plug the hole in Section 7 of the Clayton Act,[9] what has been explicitly declared to be illegal under *separate* ownership has become legal under *consolidated* ownership. High profits and intensive merger activity historically have gone hand in hand. This was true of the great consolidation movement of 1897-1905, the post-World War I movement, the period of the late twenties, and the post-World War II period in which we find ourselves. From 1940 through 1947, more than 2,450 formerly independent manufacturing and mining companies disappeared as a result of mergers and acquisitions. The asset value of these firms amounted to $5.2 billion, or roughly 5.5 per cent of the total assets of all manufacturing corporations in the country during the wartime year of 1943.[10] Consolidation was most pronounced in three branches of manufacturing: food and beverages, textiles and apparel, and chemicals, including drugs.

As of 1948, one-third of the value of all manufactures was turned out under conditions where the leading four producers of each product accounted for from 75 to 100 percent of the value of the total.

9. Section 7 prohibits corporations from purchasing stock in competing corporations if the effect would be substantially to reduce competition, but it does not forbid the purchase of assets. (This action was taken by Congress after the present manuscript went to press.—Ed.)
10. *The Merger Movement, op. cit.,* p. 17.

Moreover, no less than 57 percent of the value of all manufactures was turned out under conditions where the largest four producers in each case accounted for more than half of the total.[11]

High profits and intensive merger activity historically accompany one another. This was true in all of the four periods mentioned above. The reason is obvious: not only do profits provide the financial wherewithal with which to effect mergers, but more than that, profits exert a powerful pressure on business to expand, both internally by building new plant and equipment, and externally by absorbing competing concerns. "Like Alexander the Great," concludes the FTC report, "the modern monopolist may have to bring his merger activities to a halt, owing simply to the imminent absence of 'New Worlds to Conquer'."[12] The important social fact to keep in mind, when appraising the over-all effect of mergers on the competitive economy, is that concentration tends to become *cumulative over a period of time*. This is because each year's mergers are superimposed on a structure of economic concentration which has already been building for many years.

Defenders of the merger movement admit that dominant giants in threes and fours are a notable feature in many fields, but say that there is nothing to worry about. Competition, they claim, is often

11. *Ibid.,* p. 19.
12. *Ibid.,* p. 22. An obvious exaggeration, but sound counsel nonetheless.

even more intense where this condition exists than among scores of competitors because the few big concerns, with low unit costs, slug it out among themselves and so lower prices to the consumer. When to this plausible argument it is objected that potential power to eliminate competition is likely eventually to be used, and that the trend toward fewer units of ownership must be stopped now or never, the defenders reply that such dangers are theoretical rather than actual, and that we must wait and see. By that time, of course, as every administrator knows, it is too late. Socialism, like monopoly, is difficult to undo in favor of numerous units, individually owned, once the collective frame has been built. The only effective program, therefore, is better methods of prevention.[13]

II

Let us now take a quick look at how the battle lines are arrayed. The principal alarum comes from professional economists. Believing as they do that national resources should be allocated to various uses, that price levels should be adjusted, and that shares of the national income should be distributed *all according to the play of natural forces,* they must oppose any man-made forces that inter-

---

13. There is also the possibility of developing a substitute product or a new process which will cut the ground from under an existing monopoly. Some students of this problem have apparently concluded that this is the most promising method of providing competition once giants have become entrenched.

fere with the working of this system.[14] Oligopoly (control by the top threes and fours) is such an interference. When any business corporation, labor union, or agricultural association becomes so powerful that it can, either individually or in concert, bring about administratively what the natural forces of the market are supposed to accomplish automatically, then the system, say the economists, is being undermined and eventually will be replaced with something else.

Power to dominate the market is power to rule, and rule is traditionally the function of government. Bigness in business, therefore, takes on the character of political rule and accordingly is likely to be regarded and treated by the public in the same fashion. The problem then falls logically into the lap of the political scientist who is used to studying questions of power, rule, and administration.

Organizations of small businessmen, such as the National Federation of Independent Business, Inc., are inclined to be a little more specific about the evils of monopoly and, quite naturally, somewhat less theoretical. They complain that monopolies squeeze the life out of the little fellow, dictate prices to farmers and suppliers, reduce the margin of profit so low that the profit system itself is cor-

14. "Only pure price competition can produce the results which most people have in mind when they defend what they call in general 'the competitive system'. Non-price competition by way of product differentiation and sales promotion operates to increase costs rather than reduce prices."—Arthur R. Burns, in the *American Economic Review*, Vol. 39 (June, 1949), p. 694.

rupted for all but the largest firms, and that the big outfits gain the upper hand not because they are more efficient but because they are financially able to buy out competitors, temporarily reduce prices below cost if necessary, and weather periods of depression by living on their reserves. Small businessmen see in big business the cause of big labor and big government, all of which they would like to whittle down to size in order that they and the farmer may remain the backbone of the country. The alternative, it is argued, is some form of socialism.

On their side, the defenders of bigness have most of big business (a few are worried or have "got religion"), some articulate leaders of big labor who fear that breaking up the big corporations would result in plant rather than industry-wide bargaining, and a few, but not many, of the academic fraternity. Nor does bigness lack support from the advertising-supported newspapers, magazines, and radio. The arguments are straightforward and sound plausible. Bigness, it is said, is inevitable. If you want science and progress you must expect giantism. Bigness is peculiarly an American product and is evidence of our organizing and managerial genius. Besides, the big outfits would never have become big (and certainly would not remain so) were they not inherently more efficient; to propose seriously that they be curtailed, therefore, is to urge that they be penalized for this advantage. Only the envious or the radical, it is argued, oppose bigness; everyone else is for it because no one would pass up a chance to grow and become big himself if he could. "Big Progress and Big Business Go Together," points out the President of the General Electric Company.[15] Bigness alone is not "monopoly," he argues; a corporation is more than plant; it is misleading to emphasize "power"; small business grows with big business; and most American inventions and improvements in technology would never have been possible, at the rate they have taken place, had it not been for big business.

A curious paradox about the problem of bigness is the striking coincidence of viewpoint as between the political and economic right and left wings. The leftist position, of course, is the Marxist one which holds that bigness and concentration of power are inevitable in the capitalist system and must inexorably lead to state socialism. Once the trusts are ripe for socialization, it is said, they will be taken over by the state. But curiously enough, those who are ideologically at the opposite pole also espouse the notion of inevitability. The difference is that they attribute the inevitable trend toward concentration to the God of Technology and his twin, Efficiency. The left and the right differ, of course, in their prediction of what may be expected

15. In a 63-page brochure by that title. See Charles E. Wilson (Nov. 30, 1949), summarizing testimony given before the Special Subcommittee of the Judiciary Committee of the House of Representatives (the Celler Committee) in connection with its study of the antitrust laws. This brochure was published by the author.

once inevitability has run its course. The conservative businessman sees nothing more than a period of modified free enterprise which some euphemistically call private socialism, but certainly not public socialism; stepped-up programs of public relations can be expected to take care of that possible danger.

(Between these two extremes falls the great mass of the rest of us, those of us who believe that private ownership is better than state ownership or even ownership in a big, usually remote corporation, those of us who cherish the opportunity to start a business of our own and to make a success of it, those of us who believe that people are happier, on the whole, when business and agriculture remain small, when face-to-face relationships are possible, and when government does enough but not too much and is fairly manageable and under effective public control. In short, most of us like free enterprise of the old-fashioned sort—the kind that made it possible to start with nothing and build a lot because there were no giants already in the field to make it tough.) Now, of course, if you are one of those who has this old-fashioned view you should make up your mind immediately, say the so-called realists, that nostalgia is all you can expect. Those of the right and those of the left are agreed that the drift toward concentration and giantism must continue. Technology says so. We no longer enjoy free will because the trend is controlled by determinism.

One of the most potent arguments of the right is that since Marxists consider concentration a prelude to socialism, any who criticize the trend toward concentration must have a Marxist axe to grind. Logically, this argument is hard to support because most students of the problem are considerably more attached to the traditional concepts of private ownership than are those in big business who serve as their critics. There is an obvious difficulty here, however, in how to treat the problem constructively without becoming, unwittingly, a contributor to the Marxist dogma of inevitability. The answer seems to be that if there is any chance of saving the things worth fighting for—things like democracy and predominantly individual ownership—an energetic philosophy of free will, which has always been a pillar of democracy and freedom, must defeat the alternative deterministic philosophy of inevitability.

III

Bigness is natural and even inevitable in a culture characterized by quick advances in technology. Bigness begets power, and both size and power may be beneficial when properly used under proper controls. Under the impact of invention, corporations become large in a variety of ways. Mergers may be effected at the same level of size in order to bring about a higher capitalization or to get rid of an inconvenient competitor. The acquisition of smaller firms may be for the purpose of securing

large numbers of trained personnel. Acquisition
may also be aimed backward toward the raw material and forward toward the consumer, largely in
the interests of security. And finally there is the
purchase of unrelated lines so as to achieve diversi-
fication of investment or to provide additional out-
lets for the investment of accumulated funds. In
the 1890's for example, the General Electric Company, then in its formative years, brought together
a number of smaller firms in order to establish its
own place in the industry and to secure trained personnel at a time of expansion. Later other companies were bought so as to join related operations,
such as the X-ray, to the main body. Then during
the 1920's and 1930's, distributor houses were added
to provide more outlet channels. By whatever
means and for whatever purposes consolidations
are effected, however, the result is the concentration of power in the hands of a few companies controlled by a few individuals.

But *is* there necessarily a correlation between size
and power? The public generally assumes that there
is, and so, apparently, do most members of Congress and a majority of the Supreme Court (only
recently, it must be added).[16] On the other hand,
those identified with big business are sometimes
inclined to question this assumption, as the President of General Electric did, for example, in his

16. Cf. Wendell Berge, "The Sherman Act and the Enforcement of
Competition," Papers and Proceedings, *American Economic Review*, Vol. XXXVIII (1948), pp. 172-181.

brochure referred to.[17] Obviously it is important to determine the reliability or the fallacy of this assumption because it comes close to being central to the whole question of monopoly.

Generally speaking, the belief that size and power bear a necessary relation to each other seems justified. It does not mean, however, that there are no exceptions or that monopoly is the inevitable consequence. A small business may exercise a monopoly. A big business may not. A big business may possess a potential monopoly and not use it. Perhaps there would be less confusion in the public mind if instead of the term monopoly we used "degrees of concentration." This is an important distinction and pretty well takes care of Mr. Wilson's objections in the brochure referred to.

Power, which is a composite of factors, accompanies degrees of concentration. When a corporation can easily raise large sums of money, supply itself with the best available research brains, acquire patents helpful to itself and prevent their use by potential competitors, employ skilled executive talent at a price which smaller competitors cannot afford, effect savings due to large purchases at a discount, standardize operations due to the size and repetitiveness of the work and hence effect savings, reduce unit costs in many areas as the volume increases proportionately, weather periods of depression because of large financial reserves, operate temporarily

17. Wilson, *op. cit.;* such an assumption is "dangerously misleading," he avers.

at a loss in order to force out competition or prevent newcomers from entering the field, present a
strong resistance to labor demands which a weaker
and smaller competitor could not withstand, make
extensive use of mass communications to influence
the public favorably toward its own interest, and
have so much prestige and position that company
policies influence not only the industry but also
candidates for public office—when these things are
possible they are evidence of power (and not the
only ones, obviously) as that term is usually understood.

"Power" is a neutral word, connoting something
which is neither good nor bad. Power always means
strength. Large corporations are strong in many
forms and in varying degree. Their power may be
so great that they can fix prices which others will
be forced to follow. They may decide not to use
this power, in which case it remains potential, but
it is still there. They may be able to keep out newcomers who would like to enter the field, and in
this case also the power may be either demonstrated
or potential. In fact, power is like units of energy:
the more of them you bring together in one place,
the greater the total of energy found at one center.
In this neutral sense, there seems to be no argument that size and power are necessarily related in
a significant fashion.

But let it not be thought that unit size is the only
measure of power, which often results more from
significant *interrelationships* than from the sheer

size of separate components. There are a number of variations here. A large corporation conspiring with other large corporations obviously has more power than it would have alone because it has more influence;[18] a corporation which must decide between enlarging existing plant or going into new lines of activity may actually increase its total power more by the latter course, because it thereby increases its range of influence not only as a business-getter but also in its community and government activities. Corporations as well as individuals may therefore be rated in terms of what is called positional analysis, meaning the number of significant relationships which tend to increase the influence of the person or the social unit. Modern trends toward economic concentration are disturbing not only because units tend to increase in size, but even more because combines tend also to grow both horizontally and conglomerately. They increase their power through relationships as well as through size.

The concentration or diffusion of power has always been the central problem of institutional life, both economic and political. Concentrated power means aristocracy, monarchy, and dictatorship in government, and oligopoly (control by a few firms) and monopoly in industry. When power is concen-

18. One of the few studies of this important question, in industry, is Robert A. Gordon's *Business Leadership in the Large Corporation*, (Washington, D. C., 1945); see also Marshall E. Dimock and Howard K. Hyde, *Bureaucracy and Trusteeship in Large Corporations* (Temporary National Economic Committee, Monograph No. 11, Government Printing Office, 1940).

trated, an elite (the top few) holds the authority and makes the decisions while the majority of the people are subordinated to the will of the few, carry out orders from above, and are characteristically formed into hierarchical levels of command. When power is diffused, on the other hand, the individual determines what he wishes to do, makes his own decisions, and is free from regimentation from above. Concentration produces uniformity, diffusion encourages individualism.

The characteristic dangers of concentrated power are mistakes of judgment which have wide adverse effects, more managerial responsibility than mere humans are capable of shouldering, the appropriation of power for personal and class interests, and failure to recruit sufficient talent to keep the system operating to the satisfaction of the public. The characteristic danger of diffusion and individualism is looseness of organization which may even approach anarchy and is especially troublesome in a culture dominated by technology, which is based on order and requires careful planning and articulation of the parts.

Concentration in one area begets concentration in others. The concentration of power in industry leads to a similar concentration among workers and farmers, who must organize in order to protect their own positions in society. Since power must preserve itself, each concentration creates its own pressure groups who themselves grow in influence until eventually they are in a position to distort the operation of the free market through the use of the ordinary tools of monopoly, including price leadership, the basing point system (recently outlawed but by no means dead), control of raw materials, retail price contracts, control of patents, and the like. Pressure groups are also in a position to persuade governments to their own way of thinking. Up to a certain point, this is a legitimate function in a democracy, but it must not be forgotten that if the competition for government's favor goes far enough, one of two things may happen: government may eventually be called upon to do so much that the climate of the country becomes inimical to individual responsibility and entrepreneurship or, much worse, government may fall under the sole control of one of the power blocs, in which case freedom is replaced by class rule and possibly even dictatorship.

Another factor which helps to explain the thrust toward concentration is especially familiar to administrators: there is a seemingly inherent tendency for individual wielders of power to try to extend it. In the field of management there is a saying, "The King instinctively tends to extend his domain," and the generalization is supported by experience which is well-nigh universal. For many executives there is more deep-down satisfaction in "running things" than in other more frequently emphasized incentives, including the financial one. It appeals to his pride, satisfies the psychological craving for aggression, gives him status. The exer-

cise of power is readily rationalized and made to
appear moral: it is not for personal profit but to advance the interests of those who are dependent on
the leader, namely, employees and stockholders. To
expand is to give the appearance of being successful.
To the superficial observer it is more of a test than
internal efficiency and commendable profits. It is
a thing for which Americans, in particular, have a
passion that is often noted by people of other lands.

So viewed, the lust to grow and to expand is not
so much a "conspiracy" as a red-blooded instinct
deeply rooted in the American culture. But it is
more than that. As stated above, it is apparently
a universal tendency of administrators, and since it
is supported by strong psychological factors, it is
likely to continue to be a central factor in the
problem of economic concentration. Must we conclude, then, that at least insofar as business leadership is concerned the trend toward concentration
is inevitable? Such a conclusion might readily be
deduced, and perhaps that is the end of the matter.

As against such a conclusion, however, it can be
shown that not all administrators seek to extend
their domains indefinitely and that even those who
wield the greatest power are becoming increasingly
cautious in its use. In their candid moments (and
sometimes even before Congressional committees),
the executives of giant industries now occasionally
admit that they know public opinion must not be
defied, that their companies could easily become
larger but that they have resisted the temptation for

fear of the consequences, that if they become too large there will be a demand for socialization, for punitive government controls, and an excuse for hostility and "gouging" on the part of organized labor. Also, there are instances in which highly successful medium-sized industries have deliberately made up their minds that they have reached optimum size and have apparently had no desire thereafter to expand, even when such growth was possible.

These considerations seem to suggest that rapid and uncalculating growth may be a product of frontier periods in cultural development and that when the economy becomes older, its leaders exercise a greater caution in such matters. If this assumption is correct, then one possible solution of the concentration issue may be a change of heart and mind on the part of dominant business leadership, which in turn will be reflected in a changed attitude toward the criteria of success. Sef-restraint would then tend to buttress reasonable outside compulsion and the combination would go further in reversing the trend toward state socialism than if government enforcement were pitted against a solid phalanx of opposition on the part of big business leadership. Many would dismiss this possibility as "soft-headed idealism." To this observer, however, it seems quite plausible, and the studies of Elton Mayo, Alexander Leighton, and others who adopt a cultural approach, seem to support such a view.

IV

Basic to questions of power, control of markets and of government, and the use of pressure groups, is the problem of size. Can large size be justified in view of the ill effects produced on society, on the economy, and on government? Does it not distort the distribution of income, curb business opportunity, and dominate politics? In other words, may not size be objectionable per se so far as maintaining free enterprise and democratic government are concerned? The answer seems to be, yes it is objectionable—except, of course, where bigness is dictated by unchallengeable technological requirements. But such technological imperatives actually seldom exist to the extent generally assumed, even in the case of such industries as telephones, automobiles, and insurance. The potential power of the mammoth to control output, prices, markets, labor relations, and government, therefore, places on him the burden of the proof that size is indispensable.

The most common argument offered by monopolists and oligopolists as justification of large size is that it makes possible a degree of efficiency in management otherwise unattainable. The argument is valid up to the point of diminishing returns. There is a point in growth, for example, beyond which an organization gets out of hand, becomes too large for any one man to manage responsibly. He simply cannot know what is going on in every department, cannot see all the sub-executives he should see, and still find the time to study and direct the policy of the company for which he is primarily responsible. Nor is industry any more immune to the deadening effects of bureaucracy than government, which is more often the butt of such criticism. Furthermore, where competition has been reduced or eliminated, the incentive to efficiency is correspondingly weakened; when you know you're going to make a good profit anyway, why scratch gravel to make more?

Most businessmen today understand these managerial problems which grow out of large size and have been trying to work out correctives. So far the most promising is the discovery that much can be done by decentralizing operations among smaller plants in the field, which, however, remain tied to the parent corporation by financial and policy controls. The parent body is entrepreneur and holding company—as in the case of DuPont, General Motors, U. S. Steel, A T & T, and other industrial empires—while at the same time local superintendents enjoy as much freedom as they can hold and still meet profit schedules as set from above. It is a good formula and should be more widely used in government as in business. More will be said about this in the next essay.

But is decentralization the whole answer and is it free from hazards to business itself? The answer is no. Decentralization may improve managerial efficiency, but it does not meet the objection that financial power and control remain with the central operation, which may still allocate resources, administer prices, control and divide markets, and purchase or otherwise effectively dispose of smaller competitors. Nor does it meet the complaint of the small, independent businessman or farmer who supplies parts or products to the giant firm and finds that after becoming dependent on a contract, his legitimate profit can be taken from him almost at will. It does not satisfy the consumer either, when he finds chain stores selling below cost until competition disappears in that locality, and then boosting prices to a level that previously would have been impossible.

But this is not all. From the standpoint of the giant corporation itself the question properly arises why, if decentralization is the secret of efficiency in bigness, does not small business, under independent management, offer more advantage than holding company control, anyway, especially in view of the increasingly common use of coöperative purchasing agencies now at the service of so many small enterprises? The answer seems to be that in some fields giant corporations have advantages not available to smaller firms. For one thing, large concerns can support departments of applied research, from which comes know-how and improved technologies. Small and medium-sized industries lack the resources to employ scientists, which largely explains, for example, why a few big industries are exploiting the possibilities of atomic energy while the small and medium-sized ones are not getting in on the ground floor. It is also true that giant corporations have an advantage over small and medium-sized firms in their access to financial credits. The giants are characteristically large enough and profitable enough to be their own bankers, or, if not, they can usually float big loans on favorable terms from insurance companies and through investment bankers. In this area small and medium-sized business is handicapped, initially in getting started and later in obtaining needed capital for expansion and betterments. A third relative advantage of the giant enterprise is ability to secure valuable patent rights and to use them either in their own behalf or to restrain competition by those who might be able to afford it if patent rights were not so closely held.

Public policy almost certainly can help to repair the competitive disadvantage of smaller competitors in at least two of these areas, and it is not entirely powerless in the third. Patent laws can be amended in such a way as not to play into the hands of the would-be monopolist, and financial credits can be made more accessible to small and medium-sized business, possibly through some kind of a government-insured private loan. But when it comes to the disparity arising from research or no research, the problem is more difficult. The government can help to disseminate the results of research (as it does already in many fields, atomic energy included), but in this area big business will always and inevitably possess an inherent upper hand.[19]

19. It is not necessary, perhaps, to point out that the advantages and

What of the familiar claim that giantism results in more efficient internal management? It is doubtful that such a contention can be supported. What does seem to be correct is that large corporations, for a variety of reasons, tend to devote more conscious attention to management questions than small enterprises do, and for obvious reasons. To begin with, being large, they are faced with more institutional and human problems than their smaller competitors. Again, the giants are more "political" because, being in an exposed position due to their size and power, they face threats from government regulation, from labor union leadership, and even from socialization, which small and medium-sized businesses are either spared or which they experience to a lesser degree. A. D. H. Kaplan describes in his *Small Business: Its Place and Problems,*[20] how small business in general loses ground to big business because of weak management. If small business is to survive or even to hold its own, therefore, it must devise means of self-betterment. In other words, the causes of giantism are not wholly induced by technology nor are they due entirely to the aggressions of large corporations.

But to return to the main line of the argument. The question is, if industry can decentralize its management, why is there any limit to the size that in-

---

disadvantages just referred to apply equally to the relations between large and small governmens.

20. A study published by the Committee for Economic Development, New York, 1948.

dividual units might conceivably attain? Our first reply is that on managerial grounds the advantages of large size are often exaggerated and that the need for decentralization itself indicates that small size is inherently more efficient for unit operation.

The second aspect of the matter involves the invitation to socialization provided by monopoly under private ownership. If a business becomes so large and powerful that the public decides it should be taken over and operated by the government, world-wide experience shows that decentralization is a device that government as well as industry can use to its advantage. The literature on the subject shows that even in Soviet Russia, decentralization is a cornerstone of administration.[21] In Great Britain it is a principal emphasis of the Labour party. In most places that socialism has appeared the main effort is to give to local managers as much autonomy as possible so as to secure efficiency within a highly centralized regime.

If this threat is a real one then the leaders of giant enterprises in the United States have the most to gain from a better application of the antitrust laws, because if the present trend continues toward what many of these same businessmen refer to as private socialism, then they are likely to be the first to be affected by public socialism. On these mammoths, therefore, falls the responsibility of undermining the system they claim to support.

21. See my articles on government corporations in the Oct. and Dec. 1949 issues of the *American Political Science Review*, Vol. XLIII, pp. 899-921, 1145-1164.

So far as general political theory is concerned, the verdict seems clear and indisputable: a trend toward concentration, if long continued, eventually produces so great a monopoly of power that widespread competition and widely diffused ownership in the economic realm, as well as broadly diffused power in the political realm are automatically eliminated. This is not necessarily the consequence of deliberate design, nor is it the work of men of overweening ambition. There may be the best of good will and of good intentions. When power is concentrated, however, that is the end of the matter. It has to be defended. Gradually or precipitously, good will thereafter tends toward repression, and competence changes into bureaucracy of the objectionable kind. This is universal experience. The founding fathers of the American republic saw this truth and expressed it as cogently as it has ever been done.

What is not so clear, and what needs the immediate attention of researchers in administration, is a series of two or three questions which go to the heart of administrative theory and to some of the most vital aspects of good economic theory. What is the optimum size for greatest efficiency in various kinds of activity, both private and public? In what respects are giant enterprises relatively more efficient than small ones and in what are they inferior? Although a good deal is known about these two questions, our knowledge must be more refined and more precise.

An area which has hardly been investigated at

all, except for the fertile suggestions of Hamilton and Till in their *Antitrust in Action*,[22] is what can be done to improve the administrative and judicial methods of antitrust enforcement and what can be done to unravel and make independent again the component parts of large corporate amalgams once they have been merged. These questions are ones of the greatest urgency and studies dealing with them should be generously financed at the earliest opportunity.

V

But what does the public think about the monopoly issue and what is public opinion prepared to do about it? Here a new difficulty appears, because, although most of the teaching profession recognizes the hazards of over-concentrated power in any area, most of the emphasis in the press, over the radio, and through other channels of communication is favorable to bigness. Partly this is because the large firms are large advertisers. An outstanding example of what can be done under these conditions is the recent A & P campaign to persuade the public it is being badly treated by the federal government.

While the public remains uninformed, it is not surprising that Congress, the administration, and the courts show a certain lack of energy in strength-

22. Walton Hamilton and Irene Till, *Antitrust in Action* (Temporary National Economic Committee, Monograph No. 16, Government Printing Office, 1941).

ening and enforcing the antitrust laws. "I believe the chief reason the antitrust laws have not been more successful," says George W. Stocking, an outstanding economist, "is that no politically powerful economic group wants them to be generally enforced." Big business, he continues, "has failed to distinguish between free enterprise and private enterprise and apparently is unwilling to admit that the former is essential to the preservation of the latter."[23] Theodore J. Kreps, another authority in the field, has shown how Congress has exempted one industry or practice after another from compliance, how it has disregarded all suggestions to strengthen the law, and has failed to supply sufficient appropriations to enforcement agencies. The administration, therefore, is hampered by a lack of personnel and the staff it does have is the butt of so much contempt for "bureaucrats" and "tax eaters" that, says Kreps, "lawyers and economists of integrity, objectivity and vigorous independence of thought usually prefer almost any kind of employment to working for government." Furthermore, where the staff of the antitrust agencies may be conscientious and willing, their work is often softpedalled or undone in other divisions of the government. In the same pattern, the courts also have done their share in impairing the vigor of the antitrust laws, although here there has been some recent improvement.[24]

23. From the symposium previously quoted, *American Economic Review*, July, 1949.
24. *Loc. cit.*

If it wished, of course, an informed public could reverse this situation. If organized labor and organized agriculture were united in a whole-hearted support of a broad and effective program of antitrust enforcement, their political influence is such that with the additional help of that small but effective part of independent business which is politically articulate, they might still carry the day. Opinion polls show the attitude of labor and agriculture to be favorable to enforcement, but their support of practical measures to this end falls somewhat short of their professions of faith. Labor's lukewarm attitude is largely explained by the fact that the antitrust laws have in several notable instances been applied against them when they thought that legislatively there was no justification for such action. Farmers seem to have cooled off on antitrust as more stress has been laid on subsidies and price supports for agriculture. If psychologists and public opinion testers could be enlisted to discover just what it is that the various pressure groups want and are willing to support, it might be a useful step in clarifying antitrust enforcement.

VI

What are the alternatives that face us today in the struggle between monopoly and free competition? There seem to be three lines of development, and at least two of them offer small comfort to those who still believe in free enterprise and political democracy.

First, if the drive toward bigness, merger, and monopoly cannot be checked because there is no real desire to do so, then, according to experience in other countries, certain results may be anticipated. The antitrust laws will have the teeth still further drawn out of them. Something akin to NRA and probably going further, will be conjured up but may not last for long. Industry, labor, and agriculture will become even more powerful, more involved in politics, and more determined to secure the inside track to government; nor will business' past record of excoriating government prevent it from taking part in the scramble. Maintaining a balance among the three groups will become harder, so that one or another will eventually predominate. The group that gets to the top will then monopolize government in its own behalf and other power blocs will be relegated to subordinate positions. If this point is ever reached, then some kind of nondemocratic government will surely ensue.

When the units of industry, labor, and agriculture are many and competitive, and none dominates, popular government cannot be subverted to the use of a particular interest. But when monopoly is widespread, then government also must be controlled so that the group on top may maintain its power, both economic and political, against envious challengers. The American tradition of freedom must be supported by an economic structure which also is free, so that a man may enter his own business, maintain it so long as it is profitable and efficient, and be protected from the effects of illegal monopoly.

Otherwise our tradition of freedom and enterprise, strong as it has always been, cannot indefinitely continue. Perhaps it is true that really to appreciate what freedom and competition mean, new generations must be born into a situation where these things are institutionally possible. But can this situation be brought about, now that concentrations of power have been built so high? If the leaders of our modern power blocs were convinced of the essential correctness of this social analysis, perhaps they might be more reluctant to assume the inevitability of the race for power in which they are engaged. Unfortunately there seems to be less appreciation of what is involved in power politics than there is skill in accumulating power for the home team. It is for that reason that political wisdom is so essential in the equipment of our industrial leaders.

(The second course, if concentration goes unchecked, is a steady and unrelenting conversion of private monopolies into state monopolies, ending at last in state socialism.) The experience of Great Britain is the best recent example, but there have been others. This is not class rule, nor is it totalitarian or absolute. In Britain, labor won with the support of the traditionally conservative middle class and the coöperatives. A group of American businessmen who since World War II have studied the British situation at first hand report that monopoly in industry and commerce was among the basic reasons for the move toward state socialism in that country.[25] The only chance of reversing the trend that they can see is to adopt an effective program of anti-trust enforcement, a program which the Conservative party has been considering but apparently has not yet fully embraced.

(The third alternative, harder but more constructive than the other two, is to devise and support better methods of maintaining competition.) In the opinion of those who best understand the problem, this could be done. We need measures which are preventive, as well as those designed to deal with concentration after it has occurred. The following proposals are worth some study:

1. Give more attention and more adequate financial support to an agency of the federal government which would discover the state of competition, and conversely, of monopoly, in each important industry. Hamilton and Till underscored this need in their monograph, *Antitrust in Action,* and the proposal has received recent backing.

2. Appropriate more adequate funds for the enforcement of antitrust legislation all along the line so that prevention may receive at least as much attention as prosecution.

3. Discover more effective judicial and administrative methods of dissolving holding company amal-

25. Oral statement to the writer, by the secretary to a "Marshall Plan" group that conferred with British industrialists concerning "know how", in the early days of the ECA program.

gams and restoring competition, once a conviction has been secured, and of follow-up thereafter.

4. Prohibit mergers so as to keep firms as small and numerous as is consistent with the economies of mass production and modern technology.

5. Revise the patent laws along the lines suggested by the Temporary National Economic Committee so as to give venture capital easier access to modern inventions and technology.

6. Require federal incorporation for firms the assets of which exceed a specified minimum and which do business in interstate commerce, and limit the use of holding companies in the general business field as well as in public utilities.

7. Stabilize the general price structure through monetary and fiscal policies, but leave individual prices to seek competitive levels and perform their proper function of allocating resources and distributing income.

Specific proposals for the control of bigness in labor and agriculture have not been included in this list because it seems clear that if the problem of monopoly in business and industry could be met, the fears of workers and farmers would largely disappear and they would be more likely to support for themselves any legislation directed at the economy as a whole.

VII

In conclusion, it must not be inferred that power, either economic or political, is necessarily evil and contrary to the public interest. Power in a high tension, mechanized, technological civilization is truly inevitable. If it is *shared* power and properly distributed, and no one has too much, power is desirable and beneficial. The danger of abuse is less, individual contentment is greater, society prospers, governments remain in check.

John Locke and the Utilitarians understood that men are secure, in the last analysis, only when they own property which, by their own efforts and good management, is capable of providing them with a satisfactory living. This simple truth gains force in a society as unwieldy and complex as ours. Accordingly, economic and political concentrations, which make individual ownership so difficult that most young people today are prospective employees rather than prospective entrepreneurs, is in the wrong direction.

Private ownership and management give to society a character which no impersonal system of absentee ownership and concentrated control can ever offer: a sense of quiet confidence and security that comes when a man knows that his own efforts reflect his own personality and dreams. Ownership imparts dignity to citizenship. It should be cherished for all who have ambition. We could afford to be less efficient if it would make us more content. We could even afford to own fewer stocks and bonds if we could be sure of the satisfactions that come from owning and operating our own business. After all the technical talk of economists and political scientists, these are the things that count. Through a better balance between public and private institutions, and between individuals and groups within each institution of society, perhaps these values can be achieved.

III

THE LIMITS OF DECENTRALIZATION

IN THIS ESSAY it is assumed that the trend toward giantism in the United States will continue. Corporations, labor unions, and governments will become larger rather than smaller and the number of areas in the economy that are truly competitive will continue to diminish. If the so-called trend theory of social science is reliable as a means of prediction, such an eventuality cannot be escaped unless current directions are changed; and if the world remains in a state of warlike tension and actual hostility, the movement toward internal concentration (what Lasswell calls the garrison state) is almost a foregone conclusion.

In making this assumption, however, we do not argue that such a trend is either desirable or unalterable because trends, being subject to human motivation and control, have sometimes been reversed in human history. If we assume a continuous drift toward greater concentration, therefore, it is only in order to examine a major issue of public policy and of administrative theory that arises under a particular set of conditions which, in fact, exist today and may exist in the future.

Can the conditions underlying free enterprise and popular government be maintained under a highly concentrated economic regime? When corporations become typically large, are the inherent advantages of "enterprise" retained, or do they become lost? Are there any important differences between the managerial advantages of large corporations and large governments, or do such differences tend to shrink and even disappear with increasing size? These are the questions it is proposed to examine in the present essay.

I

The first two essays have already dealt with the general consequences of concentration on political democracy and the free enterprise system. Our hypothesis was, it will be recalled, that as economic concentration increases it becomes harder, both in government and in the economy, to maintain shared power and a balance of factors securing something like an equilibrium of forces; consequently, the dominant group is forced to assume control of both the economy and the government in order to maintain the onesided power structure that has come into being. If this hypothesis is correct, then it is important to ask how far the concentration movement may go and what may be done by management to maintain as many of the conditions of free enterprise as possible, before the system shades over into some form of either private or public collectivism.

In this essay I shall concentrate on the third factor[1] in our definition of free enterprise, namely,

---

1. See above, pp. 4, 36.

managerial freedom, because it is in this area that what is called enterprise is principally involved. Without attempting complete proof, we have already suggested tentative conclusions regarding the other two factors, namely, private ownership and competition. A brief summary of these last two points may be useful. With regard to private property, Berle and Means were the first to show rather conclusively that when, as happens under giantism, ownership is divorced from management in favor of professional managerial control, private property loses much of its original character.[2] Stock ownership is now so widely distributed that stockholders no longer have any real voice in management. Thus there arises something like the administrative state familiar to political scientists, a system in which the virtue and self-restraint of the professional managers must be relied on for satisfactory operation because popular (stockholder) control has gradually disappeared.

In important areas of the economy this situation already prevails. Even the outside board of directors, which was something akin to the separation of powers in government, has predominantly been replaced by officer boards of directors.[3] Thus policy and administration are consolidated in the hands of the same wielders of power and the outside check is lost. Stockholders must rely upon "trust" and not

2. *The Modern Corporation and Private Property* (New York, 1933).
3. Marshall E. Dimock and Howard K. Hyde, *Bureaucracy and Trusteeship in Large Corporations* (Temporary National Economic Committee, Monograph No. 11, Washington, D. C., 1940).

"control."[4] Furthermore, when private ownership loses the two important factors of participation and control, there is not much left except a chance to invest one's money and trust that it will bear fruit. Perhaps this is enough, but it is certainly a different situation from historical capitalism in which ownership and management were combined in the same hands and financial reward was justified on the ground of superior owner-manager acumen.

Recognizing this problem, the giant corporations have adopted a policy of spreading stock ownership as widely as possible. The largest public utility in the country has more stockholders—around 900,-000—than it has employees; the largest motor car manufacturer has deliberately spread stock ownership to coincide with increased labor demands and threats of federal prosecution under the antitrust laws. This is good economic strategy and it is also good politics. It takes into account what has often been observed, that frequently the holders of a few shares of stock are more conservative in their reaction to outside interference by labor and government than are the owners of large blocks of stock. The former are less secure financially and less experienced in the policies of industry.

Whether this policy of widely diffused stock ownership is an effective substitute for old-fashioned ownership remains to be seen. But two things seem clear: compared to the owner of his own property,

4. Oswald Knauth, "The Dilemma of Management," *Advanced Management,* Vol. 10 (1945), pp. 12-16.

the owner of stock is less secure because he is more dependent on others; and second, human relationships are more impersonal than formerly because the currency dealt in is pieces of paper and not the actual management of men and materials. The trend resembles that found in government because it magnifies the importance of bureaucracy and oligarchy and minimizes democratic control and individual participation.

With regard to the second element in our definition of free enterprise, namely, competition, a brief reminder may also be added here. Whether the essentials of the free enterprise system and of popular government can be maintained under conditions of increasing concentration depends on the answer to a question already raised: is so-called monopolistic competition as unworkable as it is inconsistent? Or can an economic system in which competition in many sectors has been reduced to competition between the big threes and fours continue to operate in such a way that the requirements of the free market system, namely, fluid prices rather than administratively controlled prices, will be assured? I am not competent to decide this central issue of economic theory but I must record skepticism concerning any belief that concentration and competition can be reconciled. My reason is that since areas of concentration tend to beget other areas of concentration, the effect on competition is cumulative. If the trend toward oligopoly cannot be reversed in favor of numerous units of competition,

with free access to newcomers, I must conclude
that the free enterprise system, in its essential competitive aspect, will eventually be subverted. The
balance of power in society seemingly moves one
way or the other; it does not stand still.

II

The first question to be discussed here is, can the
conditions underlying free enterprise and popular
government be maintained under a highly concentrated economic regime? In the course of studies
which I made of giant corporations between the
years 1933 and 1938, while at the University of
Chicago, I discovered that the more studious and
thoughtful executives of large corporations were
prepared even then to admit that the changed character of private ownership and the tendency for
competition to be narrowly restricted in a growing
number of areas, provided grounds for serious concern, but invariably they fell back on a panacea—
decentralization. "No problem is too great if you
decentralize enough," they would say. Bureaucracy?
Yes, it is found in every large organization, but decentralize and you get away from its objectionable
aspects. Envy and suspicion on the part of the public due to giantism? The same answer: decentralize.
Labor get tough? Decentralize. Government interfere? Decentralize. The threat of antitrust actions
to break up corporate giants? Decentralize. Internal
inefficiencies due to size? Decentralize.

But is decentralization the road to the promised

land? Can we have our cake and eat it, too? Can we, as some of these businessmen earnestly argued, enjoy the advantages of corporate power and concentration and at the same time retain that most priceless possession of the free enterprise system, the freedom and initiative arising from adequate incentives in an atmosphere which allows ability to assert itself? If we can combine the best features of collectivism (i.e., concentrated control) with individualism (i.c., freedom to be a "self-starter"), we might then have less to worry about no matter how much concentration takes place. But this provokes another question: if giant corporations may safely grow under a policy of decentralization, and if as they grow they come more and more to resemble the political state, is there not a danger that people will prove so fickle as to rely increasingly on the political state? In other words, how serious is the threat of socialism even if the internal problems of big business can be solved by improved managerial methods? Maybe if the formula of decentralization is capable of achieving as much as is claimed for it, this fear, due to the strength of the American tradition, is not worth seriously bothering about. The stakes being what they are, however, it becomes pertinent to ask: what are the possibilities of decentralization? Do they justify the seemingly extravagant claims of those who pin their faith to it?

The term has various meanings, but in industry it refers to the "geographic spreading out of a company's physical plant facilities" and to the "granting of a large degree of authority and responsibility to local plant management."[5] As used here, decentralization means particularly the centralization of ownership and the determination of objectives, combined with the delegation of internal management to local managers. Typically, the parent corporation secures the capital, carries on centralized research activities, and makes the more important policy decisions relative to product, budgets, and profit goals, while the plant manager enjoys the remaining freedoms of individual enterprise including power to formulate organization methods, operate personnel and labor relations programs, determine questions of industrial engineering, and the like. The strategy of the parent company is to give the local plant manager the feeling that, once company policies and objectives are respected, he is as free to direct the enterprise as the owner-manager of a private business in the historic sense.

A T & T, the largest nonfinancial corporation in the country, has been particularly successful in its policy of decentralization, to the extent that other large corporations consciously imitate it. The Du-Pont empire also makes decentralization the center of its managerial strategy, employing a technique that is unsurpassed by any other industrial combine. General Motors is another outstanding advocate of the decentralization philosophy, causing Peter Drucker, who reported on their methods, to claim

5. *Decentralization in Industry*, National Industrial Conference Board, Studies in Business Policy No. 30 (New York, 1948), p. 4.

that such a policy, if soundly conceived and exe-
cuted, is the solution of most of the problems of
big business attributable to gargantuan size.[6]

The National Industrial Conference Board, in its
study entitled *Decentralization in Industry*, found
that among the five principal advantages claimed
by companies with deliberate decentralization policies, "greater efficiency in smaller plants," "improved human and public relations," and "opportunity of segregating unlike operations in separate
plants" were important considerations.[7] This study,
said the report, "confirms a definite trend toward
decentralization." At the same time, although
greater unit efficiency was found to be one of the
chief virtues of decentralization, those who favored
the opposite policy, namely, centralization of plant
and operations, claimed that *in their particular industry* greater efficiency was also the ruling consideration there.[8] The inescapable inference seems
to be that in these cases—a minority—the technology
of mass production is probably the ruling consideration.

Before we go further we should understand that
the methods of concentration and corporate integration have become exceedingly complex. In discussing the possibilities of decentralization we are

6. Peter F. Drucker, *Concept of the Corporation* (New York, 1946),
   pp. 96, 119-122.
7. The other two were proximity to important new markets and opportunity to tap new sources of labor.—*Decentralization in Industry, op. cit.*, pp. 3-4.
8. *Ibid.*, p. 4.

assuming the kind of situation illustrated by General Motors in relation to the Buick Company, where both the principal and the agent are in the same business[9] and where there is a direct line of administrative authority. There is another type of case, however, where there is no top management company but merely an indirect sort of control by bankers, who may have financial interests in a variety of other undertakings. In this case the problem of decentralization obviously is different, so much so that most of the things we are going to say about administrative decentralization do not apply. Banker control is a complication faced by antitrust enforcement officials and it is also a complication for operating officials. In part, this is because professional men tend to understand and respect each other better when they have the same occupational background than when one is banker with little knowledge of the enterprise in question, and in part because there is likely to be greater sensitiveness to public attitudes and expectations when two managerial groups work together in a direct relationship than when one of them thinks only in terms of a "satisfactory" rate of return, as in the case of banker control.

Conglomerate ownership (the operation of several unrelated enterprises by the same parent company) is another development which threatens to neutralize or defeat the inherent advantages of administrative

9. This is not quite true. General Motors has some side lines like Frigidaire, but in general, it is in the motor car business.

decentralization. It is obviously easier to decentralize both *institutionally and managerially* when there is homegeniety of product than where there is hetrogeniety. The structure is also easier for the public to understand and to hold accountable. One of the great problems of finance capitalism is found right here. With the pronounced growth of conglomerate mergers in recent years, the people may not know whose product they are buying, labor relations are complicated, government's public control functions are made vastly more difficult, and problems of internal management also are greater. In addition, available evidence seems to indicate that efficiency is harder to maintain under conglomerate management, the reason being that concentration on product is the law of success for corporations as for individuals. At this point there is a striking resemblance to the traditional experience of political government. The principle is that as size and power increase, responsibility must also be proportionately increased or power is likely to be abused and management suffers because of indistinct lines of communication and control.

I shall not be surprised if eventually it is found that concentration secured by owning and controlling a number of corporations, whether related or unrelated, is considerably more subversive of free enterprise and free government than is control through sheer size in a single industry. If this prediction proves correct, the difficulty of detecting the facts of the situation and the spreading of influence (power to dominate) in a number of vital spots in the economy and in government are likely to be factors of the greatest importance.

In trying to decide whether administrative decentralization possesses the magic which is claimed for it, therefore, it must be realized that important areas fall outside the effective scope of the formula now under consideration because *in administrative terms,* banker control and conglomerate ownership present a different kind of problem. Thus it must be admitted at the outset that even if administrative decentralization is capable of solving the problems of giantism for some areas of concentration, it cannot solve the problem for all, and hence this particular formula is no panacea for the monopoly problem.

It becomes increasingly difficult to locate the situs of corporate power. For the political scientist accustomed to study the techniques of power in political institutions, the development of power techniques in giant corporations is a familiar situation. One of these techniques has already been referred to: the attempt to protect the oligarchy from unfavorable criticism by greatly increasing the number of investors in the securities of the corporation, thus tending to blur the impression of management control which exists underneath. Another has just been mentioned: the conscious or unconscious attempt to conceal the real extent of the power concentration by a complicated system of corporate interconnections, as a result of which it is almost impossible for the public to know who actually owns the brand names that are widely advertised. The corporations themselves seldom feel they have any interest in bringing this information to light and hence about the only time the extent of remote control and intercorporate connection is made available is when a hostile group such as the Federation of Independent Business, Inc., or a committee of Congress studying small business prepares charts which make the maze understandable. A great deal of such information came out of the investigations of the Temporary National Economic Committee and more recently the Federal Trade Commission's volume, *The Merger Movement*, has brought together additional facts. How many people, for example, have ever heard of the American Home Products Company? It is even less likely that the public should know that between 1940 and 1947 this single merger absorbed ten formerly independent companies in the drug and pharmaceutical field by horizontal merger and twenty-two others by conglomerate merger, or that in the latter category the subdivisions included food specialties, waxes, and polishes, chemicals, dyes and paints, insecticides, cosmetics, and a seventh, apparently unclassifiable.[10]

One of the big problems surrounding big government has always been to keep its actions under the spotlight of public knowledge and criticism; the analogous problem of "pitiless publicity" as applied

10. Federal Trade Commission, *The Merger Movement* (Government Printing Office, 1948), p. 62.

to corporate giants has by no means been solved and there does not seem to be much prospect that marked improvement is in sight. Instead, the growth of corporate concentration has been characterized by an accompanying obfuscation of identity and responsibility. Whether this policy will prove sound and rewarding, in the long run, is as much open to question as whether stock ownership, without power, is an effective substitute for the owner-manager private brand of private property. In general, it would seem safe to conclude that if public knowledge and official accountability are desirable in the case of big political governments, they are equally desirable in the case of big industrial governments. Hence it would seem better for corporations to supply information voluntarily instead of creating the impression, which is perhaps unjustified, that the extent of corporate power and its interconnections are deliberately concealed. The larger corporations become, the more they resemble political government in both internal management and accountability to the public. Wise corporation managers, wishing to retain public confidence, will therefore assume those managerial and public relations responsibilities which inhere in the situation.

III

Where there is the will to bring it about, it is surprising how much can be done to effect administrative decentralization, because almost every factor entering into management is involved in the

process. Although obviously this is not the place
to go into detail, it does seem worthwhile to list
and briefly discuss what can be done, if only because that is the one way to determine what the
possibilities of the device are, unless one is content
to accept the conclusion as an act of faith that decentralization is a panacea for most corporate ills.

Decentralization begins with provision for an outside instead of an officer board of directors, because
this makes possible a critical public viewpoint instead
of an oligarchical viewpoint, which at present is
one of the main and all too prevalent drawbacks of
the system. In other words, something akin to the
separation of powers in government, where policy
is made by one group and administered by another,
is healthy for large corporations as well as for large
governments.

In addition, the policies of the corporation
should be clearly stated and it is almost accurate[11]
to assert that the larger the corporation the more
explicit its policies should be. Here, again, the analogy to government is persuasive. When the governing and well-being of the public is importantly
affected by any institution, its "constitution" and
basic policies should be open for all to see. If it is
to live in a goldfish bowl, it is imperative that it
should be seen right. Officials of the American
Telephone and Telegraph Company have repeat-

11. Not quite accurate, because the character of the business is also
    controlling. A public utility, for example, is obviously *thought* to
    affect the public interest more intimately than, say, a company
    manufacturing chemicals.

edly told me that they attribute the managerial success of that enterprise to the fact that early in its history, due to the influence of its pioneers, the company's policies were strongly and clearly stated, so much so that they are handed down from one generation to another with little change. Moreover, when the policies and objectives are sound and can be readily understood and appreciated, they have an effect on employees' loyalty and morale that can be secured in no other way, especially if the attempted substitute is something synthetic like mere sloganizing and high-powered propaganda.

A basic rule of social psychology is that people fear what they do not undertsand and their anxiety is relieved as their knowledge increases. So long as big business is merely mysterious, therefore, it will be feared, but when more is known about it some of the apprehension is bound to disappear—one strong reason why the trend toward concealed ownership through pyramided corporations is probably not as "smart" as it is sometimes assumed to be. People know just enough to suspect that things are much worse than they are. This consideration also affects the question of opening the company books, which is a hot issue both as regards organized labor and the importunings of government. Trusteeship, by which is meant clear policies and objectives in the public interest faithfully adhered to, is good business for giant corporations.

When operating officials clearly understand what the goals are, the way is open for real decentralization. If the branch managements know enough about what the parent company expects, they can be relied on to develop the initiative and resourcefulness needed to instrument those policies; but if they are not made clear, then little further progress toward true operating decentralization should be expected.

Clearly defined objectives and policies also reduce the need for detailed operating instructions, which are one of the main causes of bureaucracy and red tape. When it takes a five-foot bookshelf of instructions from a central source to operate a field office, you can be sure that not much local initiative will be possible and that soon local managers will work according to rote instead of according to enterprise. It is important, therefore, that a sharp dividing line be drawn between general objectives and general policies on the one hand, and all the matters of internal operating organization and efficiency on the other, if units of large enterprise are to approach the efficiencies of individually owned plants of similar character. This can be done because it has been done, but it is not easy. Few corporations set a very high standard in this regard and even there, breaches of the principle enunciated are not uncommon.

Next, it is important to recruit for the highest positions in the holding company, executives who have at least two essential characteristics. First, they must know enough about social forces and social pshychology to frame sound company policies and to deal with all parties of interest. This means that they should possess all the best qualities of the best politicians—call them statesmen, if you prefer. Some American corporations call these men institutional philosophers, which is an apt designation. The second qualification is that they must have enough self-confidence and be well enough adjusted so that they will be willing to delegate as much authority to responsible operating officials as the situation requires, assuming always that the goal is that degree of administrative decentralization necessary for the release of energy and efficiency. This is no easy requirement. One of the inherent difficulties of giant corporations is that size leads to over-specialization which disqualifies top executives for the responsibilities that have been mentioned. It is small wonder, then, that large corporations frequently have to reach out to smaller companies where so-called generalists can be developed; it is small wonder, too, that giant corporations have to break away from a strict seniority principle of promotion if men with the needed qualifications are to come to the fore at the time they are needed. If we were to envisage a culture in which everything was run by giant institutions, it is probable that the leadership requirements would be next to impossible to fulfill under conditions then prevailing. One of the advantages of the independent company is that it is a better training ground for generalists than the extremely large corporation.

The question of optimum size comes next. If top executive personnel are intellectually convinced of the advantages of decentralization in terms of efficiency, they will resist the temptation to become indiscriminate empire-builders. They will wish to control those elements of the business which are essential to the success of its clearly defined objectives but they will spurn side-lines even if they are potential money-makers. Why? Because homogeniety is a law of success. Heterogeniety is characteristically less efficient. (This is one of the strongest reasons, incidentally, why governments should try to adhere to essential functions instead of trying to be all things to all people). It is not essential, for example, that A T & T should operate an electrical manufacturing business in order to run a telephone service, that General Motors should produce electric refrigerators and washing machines as well as automobiles, or that DuPont should invest heavily in automobile and tire manufacturing as well as chemicals. This kind of empire-building has no technologically justified reason, and certainly it is contrary to everything that is known about methods of securing the greatest operating efficiency. It is the weakest part of the attempted defense by big business of the status quo in response to those who would have the antitrust laws lop off such unrelated appendages.

Decentralization is also secured through a proper balance of line and staff relations. It was once thought that different personnel qualifications are needed for these two types of administrative activity, but experience indicates that a good operating official and a good staff official have more qualities in common than they have points of difference. The best balance of factors is the best combination for either type of work. If the staff man cannot talk the language of the operating official he will be ineffectual, and if the operating official cannot think out policies and procedures, as the staff man is supposed to help him do, he probably will not have very good judgment. An interchange of personnel between line and staff positions is therefore one of the best ways of holding efficiency in a large corporation. It helps to keep flexible the hard and fast lines which threaten to grow up in big organizations.

Tours of duty between headquarters and field also have a salutary effect on decentralization and efficiency. The larger the organization the greater the gulf is likely to be between the headquarters and the field points of view. This must be avoided if the outfit is to pull together. When top operating personnel are brought into headquarters for tours of duty they learn to appreciate the reasons for company policy, and when headquarters men are given operating experience they discover the field viewpoint and field problems on which sound policy must be built. Such an exchange therefore tends toward a real delegation of authority to the operating centers. Indeed, without this mutual experience it is doubtful whether effective decentralization could ever take place or real unity of operations be achieved. A T & T uses the system to great advantage, as do the armed services. One of the latest institutions to make tours of duty a cardinal principle of management, although it has experimented with it in the past, is the United States Department of State. It is a fundamental principle of management in any large institution.

Decentralization can also be furthered by wise arrrangements for supervising field offices. Examples of the wrong method are sometimes found in Washington where there has grown up a system of establishing field operation divisions heading up to a director in the home office, through whom all communications must flow. This policy is rare in large corporations and for a very good reason: it tends more toward centralization than decentralization. It also suffers from the fact that it reduces the department heads in the parent organization to the position of staff counselors with no direct line of authority to the field. It would therefore appear that if decentralization is desired, the holding company organization should render a *functional* service to the operating divisions, in which every department head is free to deal with his opposite number in the field, rather than to create an *authoritative* field operation division at headquarters.[12]

The evidence is inconclusive as to whether regional as distinguished from field offices of a large,

12. A different problem is created, of course, where there are overseas operations; then an overseas division, under a director, is usual.

nationwide organization encourage decentralization or whether they have the opposite effect. Theoretically, of course, they tend toward geographical decentralization and hence would seem to be a step in the right direction. The reason they do not always have this effect is one of human frailty: often the regional chief, fearful of his authority, will tend to invade the necessary freedoms of local operating officials, and at the same time, will keep the headquarters staff from knowing as much about what is going on in the local offices as it would know if a regional office were not interposed. It must be concluded, therefore, that regionalization may result in decentralization but that often it does not. It depends on how the system is operated.[13]

The conference technique also encourages decentralization. It is part of the process of gaining acceptance for the management's objectives and policies and is an essential aspect of public relations as well. Regional conferences, at which parties of interest are invited in, tend to cement headquarters-field understanding and to create good will. They enable operating officials to understand company policy in a way that formal communications could never make possible. It is a particularly good method in the case of programs involving social conflict situations, such as labor-management rela-

---

13. What has been said does not apply, of course, to autonomous regional authorities such as the Tennessee Valley Authority. The regional offices envisaged here are those of a single action program, such as automobile manufacturing or social security.

tions.[14] Anything that promotes understanding is an encouragement to decentralization, and thus the conference technique enables the field and the headquarters, the managers and their clients, to work out a complete relationship on a face-to-face basis.[15] Here again, A T & T has been a leader in the use of this administrative device and with outstanding results.

Sound personnel administration is another essential tool of decentralization. Personnel management, like all else, is the responsibility of the chief operating officials. Hence the top echelon should determine policy, but the administration of the program should be delegated to local executives. Personnel departments at all levels should confine themselves to staff activities and at all times should work *with* the responsible operating officials rather than independently of them or, as may happen, in opposition to them. Here is one of the areas in which the practice of the federal government has diverged most from that of industry, with results so injurious to the federal service that, since around 1938, steps have been taken to correct them. So long as top level officials determine policies, there is every reason to decentralize personnel administration as well as every other function that is involved in getting a job done as efficiently as possible.

14. For some examples, see Marshall E. Dimock, *The Executive in Action* (New York, 1945), Ch. IX.
15. Martin Kriesberg and Harold Guetzkow, "The Use of Conferences in the Administrative Process," *Public Administration Review*, Vol. X (Spring, 1950), pp. 93-98.

Financial management also goes far toward determining the possibilities of decentralization or, conversely, imposing shackles of rigidity. So long as costs are clearly and currently set forth, realistic budget estimates are prepared in advance, and effective independent audits are made, the top management has no business interfering with the autonomy of local responsible officials unless, of course, the balance sheet is unsatisfactory and then the only remedy may be a change of management. In those corporations where banker control is present and in the operations of the federal government, these principles of management have frequently been violated, with pronounced consequences in terms of impaired managerial efficiency. Finance, like personnel, is an integral part of the responsible manager's over-all responsibility and anything that weakens or divides it detracts by that much from the possibilities of outstanding accomplishment.

Public relations activities are another function which can and should be decentralized. Large corporations have found, sometimes after costly experience, that it is better policy to have local responsible officials handle law suits, hearings before government agencies, and local publicity campaigns than to centralize these activities in a remote point, necessitating the appearance of outside experts in local centers. In the United States there is, fortunately, strong resistance to outside domination and remote control. Adequate appreciation of this central fact of social psychology is a foundation stone of public relations activities. Another is the recognition that public relations grows out of institutional relationships between management and the several parties of interest. This means, for example, that operating officials should themselves deal with labor unions, instead of bringing in outsiders to perform this function. Good management, like the concentration of power, is cumulative. It is not what happens in a particular crisis that counts, but the establishment of a solid foundation for the future. There is no substitute for letting responsible management bear this burden. And it is just because owner-managers are more responsible than paid managers of large corporations and large governments that public relations (and especially labor relations) are often less satisfactorily administered in the large institution than in the small one.

IV

The potentialities of administrative decentralization are clearly impressive. Given the desire and the knowledge of principle, giant corporations and large institutions of all kinds can do a great deal to secure the advantages of small, individually-owned management among the components of a large integrated system. To conclude, however, that giant, decentralized administration is capable of maintaining a record of administrative efficiency as high as that of the best managed individually-owned corporation seems hardly justified on the basis of the known facts. Whether this is true or not depends, of course, on the criteria one is prepared to use.[16] Nor should it be overlooked that if the incentive to own one's own business continues to wane, while the appeal of a career in a large corporation steadily grows, the balance could be tipped in favor of big business management in a relatively short time. Kaplan's study of *Small Business: Its Place and Problems* indicates that the tide has been running for some time in favor of preference for the employment of college-trained men in big business, just as agencies of the federal government have been draining off the best qualified college-trained administrators from local centers for the past twenty years.[17]

Suppose we now try to strike a balance of factors, calling attention to those which favor independent business and those which enhance the advantage of large integrations. The second question posited at the outset of this essay was, when corporations become typically large, are the inherent advantages of "enterprise" retained, or do they become lost?

Owning one's business is more fun than working for someone else. This is an intangible but it is important. There is more struggle and more risk in starting one's own business and seeing it grow than in accepting a position with a large corporation on a salary basis, for entrepreneurship appeals to strong impulses in talented and able individuals.

16. The criteria of efficiency are analyzed in the following essay.
17. Morris B. Lambie, ed., *University Training for the National Service* (Minneapolis, 1932), *passim*.

Moreover, because of the nature of our pioneering culture, these impulses have been more pronounced in the United States during the past seventy-five years than in any other industrial country. There is also more independence in owning one's own business than in working for someone else, even under ideal conditions. There is more of a sense of struggle and self-reliance and more of a sense of accomplishment and well-being when successes are achieved. One's ego is nurtured by having one's own business rather than by working for the success of a corporate symbol, owned by thousands of stockholders. And often the independent business-man's prestige and position in the community are more widely respected than that of the paid exec-utive, even when the latter has a larger income.

As against these strong psychological advantages must be placed two opposing factors: first, the satis-faction of security and power which come from identification with a large undertaking, and sec-ondly, the possibility of enjoying an effective equiv-alent for the psychological satisfactions of the owner-manager by reason of skillful corporate policy. Com-petition for position is intense in large corporations and many methods have been invented to build up the prestige and ego satisfactions of big business ex-ecutives. Most important of all, perhaps, the kind of individualism which leads men to want their own business enterprises is being replaced with a type of personality which emphasizes teamwork and co-operation. The rugged individualist is the lone wolf, and there are not so many of them as there were even a generation ago. It may be, therefore, that the impact of our cultural changes is to produce an appreciation of teamwork and conformity rather than individual enterprise and wilfulness. If so, those who predict collectivism of some kind, either corporate or governmental, will doubtless be proved right in the long run.

It used to be that there was greater security in owning one's own means of livelihood than in depending on others for a job. Although this principle is still true, it is not nearly so true as it once was. Technology has changed the conditions of security as it has changed everything else. If one owns a piece of ground on which one can grow vegetables, if need be, that is a kind of security, and during the depression of the 1930's it was widespread. But that is not security in terms of the standard of living made possible by modern machines. In this context, the independent owner is as likely to lose everything if the bottom drops out of the business cycle as the man whose only reliance is on a job. In fact, the position of giant corporations is more secure in times of serious depression than that of independents. Some could close down for many months and still pay regular dividends. Accordingly, security of income-producing property is no longer the incentive it once was for independent businessmen and hence in a very real sense the survival of the free enterprise system depends on assuring enough economic stability so that the confidence of independent businessmen in the future will be strengthened.

Initiative is largely a state of mind. Of two men of equal ability, the one who *thinks* he is free will accomplish more than the one who *thinks* he is limited by inner or outer compulsions. This being the case, those who work in the employ of large corporations or other large institutions are never quite able to feel as free as they would be if working for themselves. There are a number of reasons for this. In the big institutions, men belong to a hierarchy (management group or civil service) from which certain attitudes and expectations are anticipated and demanded. The institution has rules and social observances and everyone, from the highest to the lowest, is expected to conform. The larger the organization the greater the emphasis on cooperation as contrasted with self-starting and unpredictable initiative. Try as they will, holding company executives can never give their plant managers complete freedom on everything entering into the management situation. Policies and financial results are not capable of extraction from the tools of administration: they run to every sinew and extremity of the management process. For their part, plant managers can never feel entirely free because they know there is someone higher, someone outside their immediate organization, who must be satisfied when the chips are down. They know that in every large institution there are company and personal politics, which makes them cautious and at times ruthless. This hardly adds to a sense of security and contentment with one's work.

The larger the institution the more rules and procedures it must establish and the more impersonal it therefore becomes. Individuals and their supervisors find themselves constantly fighting the impression that they are no more than cogs in a machine. Size and complexity create a sense of unreality and even mystery on the part of employees (this in varying degrees of course) which in turn create anxiety and frustration. In order to resist the unknown and the impersonal, they tend to hug themselves tightly, to become introspective. In consequence, the situation is psychologically wrong for the release of creative energy—in other words, the release of initiative. In any large organization, therefore, it seems to require more people to do the same job that fewer could do in a smaller setting.

Inflexibility of price is the aspect of bigness that the economist usually complains most about. Inflexibility of management is equally serious. The effect of large size is not only to emphasize rules of internal organization and management (commonly called bureaucracy or red tape), but also to emphasize status and organization on the part of employees themselves. In seeking security and ego satisfactions for themselves, they tend to emphasize group rights vis-a-vis management, in contrast with individual opportunities for initiative and for advancement. Guild thinking replaces individual motivation.[18]

18. This question has received increasing attention in recent years.

Large organizations are generally more rigid and less enterprising from the standpoint of internal administration than their smaller competitors, and I am persuaded that there are outside limits to what can be accomplished through constantly larger and larger doses of decentralization.

Over and against this lessened internal efficiency, however, are assets of large size which tend to repair the balance. Large corporations can afford the biggest and best machines, the biggest and best research, the biggest and best top executives, the biggest and best advertising campaigns to cover up any inefficiencies which might occur, and the biggest and best legislative representation in Washington and at state capitols. In other words, what they may lack in sheer internal operating efficiency they make up or even surpass in the instruments of power which are at their command. We come to the conclusion, therefore, that here again (and in an exceedingly important respect) there is a striking resemblance between big business and big government.

Can it be that when one gets into magnitudes of great size, the controlling factor becomes size itself and not the familiar labels of "business" and "government"? I am inclined to think that this is the conclusion that realistic analysis must bring one to accept. Which leads to where we may appropriately

---

I find Elton Mayo, *The Social Problems of an Industrial Civilization* and Alexander Leighton, *The Governing of Men,* especially revealing.

ask if there are not effective equivalents or substitutes for a widely pervasive spirit of individual enterprise. If there are, society could conceivably enjoy the advantages of bigness and at the same time not suffer any marked diminution of efficiency due to lessened initiative all along the line.

That giant enterprises have been able to compensate in large measure for the losses of initiative due to bureaucracy seems undeniable. Where do the opportunities for initiative remain? One important area is in the field of research and discovery—the introduction of new products and new processes. Here, as Charles E. Wilson claims in *Big Progress and Big Business Go Together,* the record of large corporations speaks for itself. They have well staffed and equipped research departments and their smaller competitors often have none. In the introduction of a technology as important as atomic energy, therefore, it is not surprising to learn that the big enterprises have the jump on smaller firms and that even when the Atomic Energy Commission tries to interest small and medium-sized enterprises in the industrial uses of atomic energy their efforts have been almost wholly unsuccessful. The typical response of the small manufacturer is, "I don't have researchers who can comprehend what you're talking about."[19] Large enterprises are able to afford a kind of intelligence service by means of which they benefit from the most fruitful researches of uni-

19. This information based on author's interviews with officials of the U. S. Atomic Energy Commission in Washington.

versity laboratories, while small enterprises come off a poor second. Furthermore, large enterprises have the funds and the patent attorneys to secure a corner on the market, if they wish, while their small competitors obviously have nowhere near the same resources. Insofar as "enterprise" and "technology" are equivalent expressions, therefore, the large enterprises have a decided edge.

Large corporations have a similar advantage when it comes to securing executives of talent, and in this way also they help to compensate for the loss of initiative due to size. They can go out into the open market—the market of small and medium-sized enterprise—and skim off the cream for their own use. As already suggested, however, this bringing in of new blood is eventually offset by the tendency of bureaucracy to emphasize seniority and oligarchy, so that over the long run I doubt if it can be relied on as a mean of permanently stimulating initiative and retaining comparative entrepreneurial advantage.

In another respect, however, the giants do enjoy an inherent advantage; they can secure a constant flow of ideas and initiative from their staff people, whose responsibility it is to feed a stream of ideas into the operating officials who direct the line programs. These staff people are the "stirrer-uppers," and some of the largest organizations, realizing this fact, have made highly successful use of them. Small and medium-sized enterprises, by contrast, usually give relatively less attention to the staff device and in consequence fail to benefit from the same advantages. An important principle of large-scale management is that the larger the concern, the greater is the need to underscore the inventive and enterprising aspects of staff work, in order that a flow of energy and initiative may pervade the organization as a whole and offset the bureaucratic tendencies toward inertia which are inherent.

An important qualification to everything that has been said, however, is the effect of the time factor. In the total cultural situation of the United States, large enterprises today are profiting from the benefits of a frontier civilization, when individual initiative and mobility of executive talent could be relied on because the concentration movement was still relatively new. The man with unusual energy and ability who started his small business and gravitated to the top echelons of a large corporation is the main reason that large corporations have fared so well. But what will happen if these well-springs of talent disappear? What will happen as we get further away from the frontier? What will happen if the cultural pattern becomes predominantly one of corporate concentration—a situation which in terms of vital *controls* is already here? When this condition prevails we can no longer expect the same mobility of talents to the top of large corporations. Instead, seniority and oligarchy will become more pronounced, together with greater rigidity and institutional conservatism, the end product of which is lowered initiative and enterprise. Unfortunately, there are already strong evidences of just such a development, as candid big business executives are among the first to admit.[20]

To distinguish and then add up all the factors which enter into the relative benefits to society of big versus independent business, and to do it in a manner which transcends mere individual preference and prejudice, is clearly a difficult task. That the task is worth pursuing, however, seems to admit of no question, because if society does not have a logical basis for decision-making it will drift into decisions which may be difficult to undo.

Are we as Americans in danger of losing the free enterprise system? I believe we are. And the reason we are threatened with the loss of this system is not the one which is popularly emphasized almost to the exclusion of any other. It is not the collectivist-minded bureaucrats and politicians in Washington who are chiefly responsible for what is happening, although I would not counsel less vigilance or less constructive criticism of them as individuals or as a class. The principal reason the free enterprise system is being altered almost beyond recognition is that businessmen themselves and their organizations that propagandize most in favor of free enterprise are usually the ones who unwittingly are undermining it.

20. For example, Owen D. Young once said to the author, "If big business ever breaks down of its own weight—and it may—it will be due largely to the system of seniority promotions, which discourages inventiveness and progress."

Why? Most businessmen are honest and straightforward. Once you know them you lose any suspicion you may have had that they are hypocrites, talking free enterprise but knowingly acting contrary to its interests. The explanation is found somewhere else. First, until recently,[21] they were so busy with their own corporate responsibilities that few felt they had the time to think in terms of what is happening to the economy as a whole. Second, and this is the point I want to underscore, as a group, businessmen have not thought consecutively about certain factors that they (unwisely, it seems to me) dismiss as "theoretical." My belief is that these factors which are so blandly brushed off, actually control the future of the free enterprise system.

These factors are the need to look ahead and get a time perspective; the need to view industry from a broad cultural standpoint, giving consideration to the future of free government, for example, as well as to the freedom of stock market operations; the need to examine critically the inevitability theory of social movements; and the need to accord adequate weight to the consequences of external factors, particularly war and military expenditures. Now maybe it will be objected that businessmen do give these factors the attention they deserve, in

21. The situation has changed in many corporations, not because executives are less busy but because specific provision is now often made for "generalists" to handle matters of institutional influence and survival. This is usually the job of the president or the chairman of the board, in which case an operating vice-president may be responsible for handling internal administration.

which case I would be only too glad to admit that I am mistaken.

Let us consider the four points just made. Businessmen cannot be blamed for thinking that a *certain amount* of concentration is inevitable, because technology is partially responsible and technology is desirable. But they can be criticized for undermining the system they favor when they fail to ask, "Is it technology or something else?" More often than not it is the latter. It is an immature rambuctiousness that makes some men want to accumulate power in order to feel big. Big plants for standardized products? Of course. Assembly lines? Same answer. No one that I know of seriously questions this form of bigness. But how about conglomerate mergers? Or vertical and horizontal mergers carried to excess? How about Western Electric, Frigidaire, and a host of others? How about banker and holding company control of businesses that suffer from lack of managerial independence? Are these things justified in terms of private ownership, competition, or managerial freedom? I don't see how they can be. They are a greedy quest for power and influence. They convert the free enterprise system into a political government and will eventually lead to socialism.

The difficulty of convincing businessmen as a class that this is true is that more often than not their rejoinder is, "But it hasn't happened *yet*," usually adding under their breath, "And it won't, if we can get rid of that d--- outfit in Washington!"

But the word "yet" is the crux of the matter. If American businessmen were class conscious or if family traditions in business were strong (for the absence of both of which we can, on most counts, give thanks), then more businessmen would doubtless pay greater heed to the morrow. Or if they were really convinced that you can't have your cake and eat it too, they might act differently—meaning by this figure of speech that they seem to think they can gradually but steadily stifle competition and still have private ownership and freedom of management. Fortunately for the future of the system, there are some farseeing business leaders who do appreciate the peril and are trying to do something about it, both in their own businesses and in influential business associations to which they belong. There would probably be more such men if only they understood better what needs to be done.

The hope of saving the free enterprise system lies in big businessmen's stopping short in their tracks and saying, "If concentration progresses as fast in the next thirty years as it has in the last three decades, the free market will be a thing of the past. Competition is essential and it can be restored." Frankly, I am not at all sure that they will say this until they have had their fill of oligarchy and monopoly.

The second factor mentioned above and which most businessmen tend to dismiss as "theoretical," is the need to adopt a broad cultural viewpoint. Here a lesson is to be learned by some of us academic specialists as well as by the big businessmen we sometime criticize. I doubt whether the case for free enterprise will stick so long as it is confined to "purely" economic questions such as the self-regulating market. It is too easy to dismiss this argument with the statement, "Market, hell, all I want to do is make money." But with a broader cultural approach it can be seen that people are happier when they own their own means of livelihood than when they are but cogs in a vast machine; that widespread ownership of property develops independence, pride, and individuality, values worth striving for in any social system; that people seem to work harder and better for themselves (or for the in-group, as the social psychologists call the social grouping within formal organization) than they do for a lifeless collective label; that there is less danger of power being abused if it is widely distributed than if it is highly concentrated; that men, like animals, run faster alone than when tied to a twenty-mule-team; that balance is the secret of well-being in society as with individuals and that if history proves anything it is that free or popular government depends on recognizing all organized groups and allowing none to dominate.

Perhaps a clarification of terminology will help. Concentration of economic power is collectivism. Socialism is a form of collectivism. So is concentrated corporate power. Our economic system does not retain the essence of free enterprise simply because it grew out of a laissez faire cultural background. The system becomes something else, collectivism. Collectivism is rule by large powerful groups. Once it occurs in the economy, there is a relatively simple transition to collectivism in the political state.

Many businessmen apparently doubt this. They fall back on what they call the American "genius" or the American "spirit." There is such a thing, to be sure, and it must be preserved and strengthened. But it will disappear unless the economic organization of society makes it possible for new generations to grow up under free and competitive conditions. Already the changed attitude may be noted amongst those who were born to depression, wartime economic planning, and corporate collectivism. They do not prize traditional American economic freedoms as highly as did their grandfathers because they can no longer experience freedom and competition in their full vitality.

The third factor mentioned above is the inevitability theory, which seems to be accepted equally by both big business and by extreme left-wingers. Many big businesses are engaged in selling the American public on the notion of inevitability—note, for example, Peter Drucker's article in the June, 1950, issue of *Harper's Magazine,* or Charles E. Wilson's philosophy in *Big Progress and Big Business Go Together.* This policy is explained, no doubt, by a feeling on the part of big business that it is on the defensive against antitrust prosecutions; but the net result, if successful, is to sell the American public on still greater concentrations of economic power. This may serve the immediate self-interest of the particular corporation but what will it do to it and other corporations in a generation or two? The stock answer is, "Businessmen have never looked ahead and they never will." If so, they have failed to learn what every ruler in history has had to learn, often the hard way: that with power there goes a commensurate responsibility; neglect it, and you are heading for a loss of that power to someone else. The best course, therefore, is to distribute power as the free enterprise system and political democracy have traditionally tried to do.

It might be possible to concede some of the above arguments, say the defenders of corporate collectivism, and still fall back on an argument that defeats the opposition: big wars can be fought only by big corporations and hence we should be thinking about national security and not about competition. In terms of expediency this argument has merit, though not as much as is sometimes claimed for it. With careful advance planning, the resources of small and medium-sized enterprises may provide a potential as great as that resulting from contracts exclusively with large corporations. As a long-range proposition, however, big business should reflect that the costs of total war will destroy their prosperity and freedom along with that of everyone else, if destructive wars are continued long enough. There seems to be no escaping the conclusion, therefore, that the free enterprise system can survive in the indefinite future only if a solution is found, in time, for the problem of world security. Peace and free enterprise are synonymous.

This may be theory. But theory that is posited on cause-and-effect relationships is as realistic as the routine operations of the businessman's work day.

VI

We come now to the last of the three questions asked at the outset. We want to know if the factor of bigness tends toward the disappearance of important differences between private and public management. Or, putting the same question another way, do business and government increasingly resemble each other as they become large? My answer to both of these questions is, yes. But in making this reply I am simply echoing what countless businessman have learned through experience in Washington during World War II.

From close observation, both in their own company and in the government, many businessmen now know that as corporations and governments alike grow in size, more attention must be given to the problem of power in terms of influence and survival; that "diplomatic" relations occupy the center of the top officials' attention because labor, government, stockholders, and consumers, or other bureaus in the case of government, must all be kept happy and their rival claims balanced; that the larger the organization becomes the more pronounced are its

bureaucratic characteristics; that these are inherent
and due more to the size than to the nature of the
enterprise; that the larger the enterprise becomes
the greater is the demand on top executive talent,
the greater the need for decentralization, and for
skillful staff organization; that "civil service conditions,"—meaning hierarchy, job classifications,
regular promotions, seniority—characterize both big
business and big governments; that traditions and
ways of doing business tend to become deeply entrenched and correspondingly hard to change; that
employees all along the line are inclined to lose their
individuality and become conformists and that the
larger the organization, the greater is the tendency
to create groups within groups, accentuating syn-
dicalist activity and social cliques as the expression
of an instinctive search for security against the
power of management as well as relief from sheer
boredom.

Big business and big government both experience
the common difficulty of providing effective incentives in order to get the best out of their employees. A guild spirit grows up which is the opposite of entrepreneurship and self-started propulsion.
Paid managers attach their loyalties first to the man-
egerial guild and only second to their employers.
Management becomes a game instead of something
in which a man has a direct personal stake. The
prizes are prestige and position, and profits are
chiefly important as they contribute to these two
goals. Such paid executives are inclined to look

complacently on what they call civil service conditions because their guild is a part of the system and their influence is due in large part to their having influence with the other groups constituting the hierarchy. Imperceptibly but surely, executives and employees alike lose the sense of strenuous competition and think increasingly in terms of doing the particular job assigned to them. The organization is so large that it is hard to see the end product and goal of individual effort. One becomes a "career" man.

Problems of mixed loyalties arise. The top management has to work harder than in a smaller enterprise to attach employees' loyalties to a single institution, the business or the government department. A common problem is that people seek to serve themselves instead of the corporate symbol or the public agency of which they are a part. They do things that are aimed at getting promotions even when such actions are not always in the best interests of the enterprise as a whole, and especially in support of its long-time interests. This is partly due to the fact that being small parts in a big machine, men feel that their actions are less subject to steady scrutiny from above. The internal "politics" for position and influence also seems to vary with size, one reason being that individuals feel they must contrive harder to be noticed lest they be swallowed up in the conglomerate mass.

The importance of measuring devices is another factor which varies with size. The large enterprise is the stronghold of experts of all kinds, especially the industrial engineer and the efficiency expert. Size complicates the industrial problems of personal observation, supervision, and control. Substitutes must be found and these take the form of quantitative criteria of efficiency, entailing standardized procedures and the measurement of all results that are measureable. The importance of financial administration also magnifies, for these are the gauges the top executive must watch as a fireman watches the gauges on his boiler. The net result is that standardization and measurement lead inexorably toward centralization despite the fact that decentralization, as explained, is the goal that must be sought if greatest operating efficiency is to be attained.

Where the concentration ratio is high, as in telephones, aluminum, or the Post Office, tests based on the open market and profit and loss tend to be replaced by internal comparisons of unit performance. The free market is no longer an effective regulator of price or of efficiency. Thus, top management must provide substitutes for external competition in the form of internal competition. Everything subject to measurement is made a yardstick for judging the output of units of organization doing the same kind of work. One operating company in the Bell System is compared with all the other operating companies in the same system; postal costs in New York City are compared with those in Chicago; the costs in aluminum plants in the south are compared with those in the north. Managerially determined efficiency becomes an inevitable substitute for prices set in the competitive market. The man with a stop watch or a slide rule becomes more essential than the plan of impersonal forces in the market. Decision-making is transferred from the front office and away from the higgling of the marketplace.

Consequently, in comparing large private and public institutions, size becomes the determining factor. The smaller the unit of private management, the greater, as a rule, are its points of difference from the typical governmental management of similar size. The larger the unit of private management, the more similar, as a rule, are its points of resemblance to typical governmental management of similar size. This does not mean that there are no differences, for obviously there are. It simply means that the bigger a corporation grows, the more like political government it becomes.

What are the differences between a business enterprise and a government agency? There are three, principally: more emphasis in business on profits, decentralization, and public relations. But the important thing to note here is that all of these emphases *may* also be used by government enterprises when the community effectively desires that they should. Government ventures may stress profit-making and many of them, especially outside the United States, already do. Similarly, they may relax central financial and personnel controls and adopt organizational devices for securing the greatest amount of decentralized administration, which is one reason why the government-owned corporation has been so extensively used throughout the world in recent years. There is also ample evidence that public agencies may make wide and effective use of public relations programs when public opinion favors such a course, a good example being the operation of the British telephone system by the British post office.

In mentioning these factors I must not be understood as favoring widespread public ownership of economic enterprises. On the contrary, my belief is that modern governments are in danger of trying to do too much. They should emphasize economic stabilization, not business operations. The best governed society is one in which power is wisely distributed between public and private responsibility, each doing its appointed task, a society in which power is broadly distributed between private ventures, none becoming so large as to undermine the competitive system. This is my preference as well as my belief and these, in my opinion, are sound policies to be followed.

However, I cannot escape the conclusion that just as the requirements of war-time demands constitute the clinching argument of pro-big-business advocates, so the threat of socialism is the rebuttal of those who oppose the uncritical acceptance of the inevitability theory. When big business becomes too big it becomes so much like big government that there is little to choose in the way of differences of organization, management, and over-all efficiency. People do not need to be told this. They observe it. The way is therefore paved for transferring large units of private enterprise to the public enterprise category.

The American people would be well advised to give due warning to monopolies and near-monopolies that have grown unjustifiably large. That is the best way, and perhaps the only way, of awakening them to the virtues of private ownership, competition, and managerial freedom, all of which are essential to the continuance of the free enterprise system.

IV

THE EFFICIENCY CONCEPT[1]

To win an argument with an American you have only to convince him that what you advocate is efficiency. In the American culture of the past fifty years, no claim to support has been received more sympathetically.[2] Soon after the turn of the century, efficiency came to be regarded as a "Gospel"[3] and the lack of it almost a crime.[4] The fact that the term covers so much and is so hard to pin down has proved a positive advantage in terms of its popular acceptance. Today efficiency is a religion with its full complement of ministers and acolytes. "If cleanliness is next to Godliness then to be efficient is just one step behind in the eyes of most American citizens. We gauge our very living upon this magnificent method of measurement. Is this an efficient machine? Is that an efficient schedule? Plans, processes, ideas, organizations—

1. In writing this essay I have drawn on the work of some of my graduate students in a seminar conducted at Occidental College during the winter of 1949-50. Outstanding papers on the concept of efficiency were written by Messrs. Wallace H. Best, Marshall C. Johnson, and John Penney.
2. Dwight Waldo, *The Administrative State* (New York, 1948), pp. 19, 60.
3. "The Gospel of Efficiency" is the title of a chapter in Harrington Emerson's book, *Efficiency as a Basis for Operation and Wages* (New York, 1909).
4. Best expressed, perhaps, in the *Preface* to L. Urwick, *The Elements of Administration* (New York, 1944).

nothing is safe. If time can be saved, movements eliminated by some new approach, the inventor is a hero in the eyes of his countrymen. But let an accusation go unchallenged that you are inefficient—well, you might as well pack up your bags for Laborador."[5]

Of the many interesting phases of this new religion,[6] none is more significant or timely than the one that makes efficiency the bulwark of bigness and concentrated economic power. The claim that they are more efficient than smaller competitors and that they are entitled to the same freedoms as everybody else, says David Cushman Coyle, are the twin arguments of giant industries designed to appeal to the entrenched attitudes of the masses.[7] In his treatise, *Big Progress and Big Business Go Together,* the president of General Electric relies on the efficiency argument more than any other: "It is a commonplace that without the efficiencies of size and large volume production the luxury that is the automobile could not conceivably be made available to so many millions of people." Or, again, "The impact of this mass production efficiency when translated into war power is too well known and of too recent demonstration to require recalling here." Further, he argues that workingmen would never

5. Marshall C. Johnson, "Efficiency in Administration," unpublished thesis, above referred to.

6. On the historical aspect, see B. P. DeWitt, *The Progressive Movement* (New York, 1915); Chapter 15 is entitled "The Efficiency Movement."

7. See his article, "The Big Cannot Be Free," *Atlantic Monthly,* Vol. 179 (June, 1947).

have been able to realize their present high level of wages if it had not been for giant corporations.[8]

The inference is clear: to consider passing legislation restricting giant corporations is to vote against efficiency, a high standard of living, adequate preparation for war, and high wages for labor.

What is efficiency? Is it as all-inclusive and all-satisfying a concept as past usage would make it appear? How did this passion for efficiency become so deeply imbedded in American folkways? How accurate a yardstick is it in deciding public policy issues, such as whether giantism or competition is to be preferred? And is the term overworked and in need of sharper differentiation?[9]

I

Theoretically, efficiency is a purely abstract and colorless word, meaning simply the ratio of results achieved to the means used, or the highest level of output for energy and talent expended. Actually, however, as we all know, efficiency means a bewildering variety of things and its uses have con-

8. Charles E. Wilson, *Big Progress and Big Business Go Together* (brochure, privately printed, 1949), p. 15.
9. I have written on the subject of efficiency previously and since that time have not appreciably changed my ideas. It is to be hoped, however, that my thinking has broadened and deepened. If any excuse is needed for writing on this subject again, it is that I now want to relate it to the pivotal question of corporate giantism and the drift toward collectivism. See my chapter, "The Criteria and Objectives of Public Administration" in *The Frontiers of Public Administration* (Chicago, 1936), by John M. Gaus, Leonard D. White, and Marshall E. Dimock.

stantly grown as the concept has become increasingly pivotal. One student has concluded that "There is then no such thing as efficiency *per se*; there are rather many kinds of particular efficiencies," a conclusion which will hardly surprise the modern student of semantics. The term itself, he continued, means "nothing" and is of consequence only as a ratio relating results to input.[10] Although from a coldly logical standpoint this conclusion is undoubtedly correct, from the standpoint of the pragmatic uses to which the concept is nowadays put, it is of the utmost importance; in its effect on public attitudes and policies the term efficiency today probably means as much as any word in the American language.

Sumner Slichter believes that the pattern of efficiency includes at least three particular kinds: (1) engineering or physical efficiency, which is the relationship between physical quantities consumed and produced; (2) pecuniary or business efficiency, which is the relationship between dollars spent and income obtained; and (3) social or human efficiency, the relationship between the human costs incurred and human satisfactions or benefits produced.[11] Although this is a good working outline it is not free from problems of classification. From the point of view of the businessman, for example, efficiency means a method of production yielding

10. Wallace H. Best, unpublished thesis above referred to.
11. In his article on "Efficiency" in the *Encyclopedia of the Social Sciences,* Vol. V, p. 437.

the largest output at the lowest money costs, but from the workman's standpoint it means a method yielding the largest output at the lowest human costs in terms of fatigue, monotony, accidents, and the like. Both are elements entering into the "pecuniary or business" equation, but they are also obviously involved in the other two categories, the engineering and the social.

A study of the history of the expansion of the term in the American habitat shows that in the early part of the present century the engineering and business aspects were emphasized primarily, whereas in more recent years increasing attention has been paid to the social aspects of efficiency. And since "social" is the broadest and most expansive of the three connotations, it is a clue as to why the term has taken on such a variety of meanings. Some prophetic souls, like Harrington Emerson, envisaged the broad concept which would eventually emerge, and did so early in the twentieth century: "Efficiency," he said, "means that the right thing is done in the right manner, by the right men, at the right place, in the right time. True efficiency means ameliorating conditions for the workers, both individually and collectively—not only for the employer, but also for the corporation, and finally for the nation."[12]

---

12. Harrington Emerson, *The Twelve Principles of Efficiency* (New York, The Engineering Magazine, 1912); cf., by the same author, "Efficiency Engineering," *The Encyclopedia Americana* (New York, 1949), Vol. 7.

The engineering profession, and particularly that group called efficiency engineers, pioneered the concept of efficiency in the American culture. From the outset they seem to have taken a surprisingly (for that time) broad view of what is entailed in "management," "principle," and "efficiency." Said Frederick W. Taylor, "The best management is a true science, resting upon clearly defined laws, rules, and principles, as a foundation. . . . The fundamental principles of scientific management are applicable to all kinds of human activities, from our simplest individual acts to the work of our great corporations, which call for the most elaborate coöperation."[13] In an attempt to be scientific, they sought "the best way" of doing everything involved in coöperative effort. According to Harrington Emerson, efficiency is a word of comparatively modern use, for which there is no equivalent in French, Italian, Russian, Swedish, or German; it can be defined as "the industrial relation between what is and what ought to be, between the actual and the standard."[14] The "one best way" point of view has sometimes been criticized for its seeming dogmatism and its failure to take account of all the philosophical factors involved,[15] but in fairness it should be recognized that the pioneers in the field early saw the broader implications of the

13. Frederick W. Taylor, *The Principles of Scientific Management* (New York, 1919), pp. 5-7.
14. Emerson, "Efficiency Engineering," *The Encyclopedia Americana, op. cit.,* p. 716.
15. Dwight Waldo, *The Administrative State* (New York, 1948), p. 59.

problem and took steps increasingly to deal specific-
ally with the social and human aspects of the effi-
ciency-management concept.

When Harrington Emerson said in 1912, for example, that "Efficiency engineering is immediately
concerned with industrial wastes and not with moral
wastes,"[16] it is clear from the total reading and from
the insertion of the qualifying word "immediately,"
that he was merely trying to limit his area of in-
vestigation, as any scientist would. But that he was
also concerned with human elements is shown by
his emphasis on such factors as "the fair deal" and
"efficiency rewards."[17]

As one reads the outstanding articles in *Advanced
Management* and its forerunner, *The Bulletin of
the Taylor Society,* one cannot help but see in the
positions of Harlow Person, Wallace Clark, Ordway
Tead, Morris L. Cooke, and others, a recognition
of the fact that efficiency is an increase in productiv-
ity, coupled with the lowest possible cost involved,
but also including the human element of satisfaction
in all stages of the economic process. Merely read, for
example, Harlow Person's excellent article on "The
Genius of Frederick W. Taylor,"[18] or the symposium on scientific management which appeared in
1940,[19] and it will be clear, I think, that the concept

---

16. Emerson, *The Twelve Principles of Efficiency, op. cit.,* p. 59.
17. Emerson, "Efficiency Engineering," *The Encyclopedia Americana,
op. cit.,* p. 718.
18. *Advanced Management,* Vol. 10 (1945), pp. 2-11.
19. *Ibid.,* Vol. 5 (Oct.-Dec., 1940).

of efficiency has been constantly humanized by the skilled group which first gave it prominence.

II

What does efficiency mean in terms of the second category differentiated by Sumner Slichter, the pecuniary or business category? This is particularly interesting from the standpoint of shedding light on the claims of giantism to superior efficiency. To distinguish all of the criteria of efficiency in the industrial realm—not to mention other areas of the economy—is obviously beyond the reach of this paper and hence we must be content to hit only the high points and to confine ourselves to what some of the outstanding students of the subject have uncovered.

A leading economist has differentiated twelve variables governing productive efficiency:[20]

    (a) The proportion between different productive factors

    (b) The percentage of the full capacity of the plant which is utilized

    (c) Steadiness or fluctuation in the rate of output

    (d) The number of units produced of a given size, type, brand, or model of goods in a given plant

    (e) The proportion of different products turned out by some central process or plant

20. John M. Clark, *Studies in the Economics of Overhead Costs* (Chicago, 1923), pp. 79-83.

(f) The size of the single plant

(g) Integration or vertical combination

(h) Horizontal combination

(i) The extent of competition or monopoly

(j) Geographical concentration of industry

(k) Geographical density of population and industry in general, in its effect on the general efficiency of the economic system

(l) Degree of coöperation between industries of different sorts, and different industrial groups or' classes

The author explains that there is a reciprocal relationship between the extent to which the capacities of different factors are utilized, that often one factor can be fully exploited only at the expense of another, and that economies result from developing the unused capacities of productive factors.[21]

The factors listed above relating to size are of particular interest here. Although the giant firm may reduce cost per unit, to a point, by increasing input or by organizational integration or concentration, the fixed charges involved are usually very large and rigid. On the other hand, "The average small business seems to have ample leeway for utilizing its personnel and facilities to better advantage at the expense of only a slight increase in costs."[22]

In the industrial realm as elsewhere, efficiency means different things to observers in different po-

21. *Ibid.*, pp. 72-73.

22. A. D. H. Kaplan, *Small Business: Its Place and Problems* (New York, 1948), p. 102.

sitions. To the business manager, who in our modern corporate structure is more often agent than owner, efficiency traditionally means maximum production at the lowest possible cost combined with maximum returns to the owners of invested capital. Unfortunately, however, through a variety of circumstances adverted to in previous chapters, these two ends have often come to be more nearly dichotomous than complementary. As explained by Peter Drucker, "the corporation's criterion and yardstick of institutional efficiency, profit, and society's criterion of economic efficiency, maximum producton at the lowest cost," frequently need reconciling.[23] Accordingly, the role of the manager is to distribute power and responsibility, to formulate general and specific criteria of policy and action, and to select and train leaders so as to utilize to the utmost all of the resources, both human and material, of the corporation, to the end of maximizing profits and satisfying other parties of interest. The manager's efficiency is to be judged by the extent to which he achieves this goal, coupled with economical production and the continued successful survival of the corporation as an institution.[24] This last point is a crucial proviso and leads directly to some of the most important questions surrounding the third category, the social tests of efficiency.

As viewed by the stockholder, efficiency is a maxi-

23. Peter F. Drucker, *Concept of the Corporation* (New York, 1946), p. 210.
24. *Ibid.,* p. 40.

mum return on investment. It may be computed directly as a percentage, a measurement which, when possible, is the best approximation to accuracy.[25] Since the stockholder's primary and natural interest is pecuniary gain rather than the production of goods and services, usually he is concerned only with profits, however derived, and will condone scarcity and monopoly practices where he profits by them even when they run counter to his interests as consumer or impair industrial efficiency, in the productive sense, as well as the maximization of real wealth for all.[26] This kind of analysis could be carried further, but perhaps enough may have been said to open up the question that chiefly interests us—the concept of efficiency as applied to large size.

Just as the law of diminishing returns applies in certain areas of economics, so also the law of optimum size apparently applies in the realm of institutions. In terms of managerial operations, efficiency seems to increase with size up to a certain point, but thereafter it falls off for each additional unit of size. Furthermore, once the optimum has been exceeded, the efficiency of the entire enterprise is likely to be adversely affected.[27] The point

25. Vanderveer Custis, *The Foundation of National Industrial Efficiency* (New York, 1923), p. 22.
26. Clarence J. Foreman, *Efficiency and Scarcity Profits* (Chicago, 1930), pp. 318-320.
27. This subject has received a good deal of attention in the literature of scientific management. In addition to the publications of the American Society of Mechanical Engineers, consult, especially, the work of Harry A. Hopf, who has written extensively on optimum

at which the optimum occurs, differs, of course, in different industries and in different institutional processes.

Even more than engineers, professional economists are becoming increasingly concerned with the proper relation between size and efficiency, so that today this issue is considered of primary importance in the future growth of economic theory. Every annual meeting of the American Economic Association since the conclusion of World War II has dealt either squarely or indirectly with the basic problem, and the reader will find of particular interest the papers and proceedings appearing in 1948 and 1950, respectively.[28]

Generalization on any subject containing so many variables obviously is fraught with danger of over-simplification,[29] and yet amongst both economists and management engineers there is wide agreement on the essentials. Kaplan, in his book, *Small Busi-*

---

size in the *Bulletin of the Taylor Society* and *Advanced Management*. A great deal more needs to be done. For several years the Federal Trade Commission has sought funds from Congress with which to make intensive case studies, but not enough have been forthcoming. This is an area where some of the larger privately endowed foundations could invest funds profitably.

28. "Does Large-Scale Enterprise Result in Lower Costs?", Papers and Proceedings, *American Economic Review*, Vol. XXXVIII (1948), pp. 121-171; and "Capitalism and Monopolistic Competition," *Ibid.*, Vol. XL (1950), pp. 23-104.

29. "The literature of economic concentration," says A. D. H. Kaplan, "has waxed progressively cautious about treating the size of firm as an independent variable. . . . Absolute size has proved less meaningful than relative size for determining the influence of a single firm or group upon market structure and behavior."—*Ibid.*, p. 74.

ness: Its Place and Problems, devotes a chapter to the influence of size on the efficiency of business. He points out that "The middle-size firms of an industry commonly make a better average showing on costs and earnings than do either the giants or the smallest members." He goes on to say further, that "The over-all tendency is for unit costs to diminish as size increases until the big business category is reached, but the very largest member of an industry does not usually show the lowest cost or the best profit rate on invested capital—in most cases a firm in the middle range makes the best showing, and frequently a small firm leads the industry in this respect."[30]

The colossus of the steel industry, United States Steel, is a good example of the validity of these generalizations. The hearings before the Celler Committee of Congress, relating to monopoly power, says Inge Kaiser, a former employee of the War Production Board, "went far to demolish the myth that bigness automatically means efficiency."[31] The president of United States Steel told the Celler committee that the efficiency of large corporations does not require the attention of Congress. "I do not think the Congress of the United States needs to worry about that," he said, "because that fellow

30. A. D. H. Kaplan, *Small Business: Its Place and Problems* (New York, 1948), p. 80.
31. See his article, "A Hard Look at U. S. Steel," *The New Republic,* April 21, 1950, p. 14, which is replete with significant data and comparisons arising out of the testimony of U. S. Steel officials themselves.

[the inefficient corporation] will go out of business automatically, because of our great competitive system." But Mr. Kaiser's comment was that "The Corporation's own history, as disclosed in these hearings, disproves Fairless' theory. While a small business needs to be efficient, a large, well-entrenched, economically powerful industry can continue merrily in business even though inefficient."[32] He added that on the basis of information contained in a report instigated and paid for by the Corporation itself, such a conclusion is inescapable.

The public's dilemma in making up its mind about this issue is explained by the engineer, David Cushman Coyle, who designed skyscrapers before he turned writer. Middle-sized things are not news in America. "All through the nineteenth century and down to date, science and invention have been piling up examples of the value of big machines, big factories, and mass production. . . . In some lines of production . . . larger operations turned out more goods for less money, compared with the smaller productive units they displaced. . . . How could the public ever guess that the big plant is only sometimes more efficient, or that in most industries the middle-sized plant works better than either the small or the big."[33]

The available evidence seems to indicate that bigness, *per se,* is not necessarily efficient from any

32. *Ibid.,*
33. David Cushman Coyle, "The Big Cannot Be Free," *The Atlantic Monthly,* Vol. 179 (June, 1947), p. 78.

of the three standpoints examined, the engineering, the economic, or the administrative. What is commonly thought of as efficiency is often concentrated power, which gives its owner staying power.

III

It was remarked early in this chapter that social or human efficiency has been increasingly emphasized, in contrast to engineering and industrial efficiency, as the twentieth century has progressed. This is not surprising if one believes, as the present writer does, that the cultural view of human relations has the most to offer to the student of the social sciences. In its simplest form, says an authoriy on economic efficiency, national productive efficiency is "the ratio of wealth produced to the human energy and the natural resources utilized in the process."[34] This sounds like a true and logical statement, and yet, almost at once it is apparent that it leaves out of account many important factors entering into national strength and greatness. What is the effect of efficiency on people, morals, aesthetics, general contentment? Must we be satisfied with two brands of economics, the purely productive and the more broadly social, or is such an assumed dichotomy unnecessary and unsatisfactory? Or applying the same test to the field of administration, is there one science which concerns itself only with process, and another broader body of knowledge dealing with

34. Vanderveer Custis, *The Foundations of National Industrial Efficiency* (New York, 1923), p. 4.

philosophy and values? It seems clear to one interested party, at least, that the best and most lasting results will be secured if instead of a dichotomy we work toward a realistic synthesis. It is a source of encouragement, therefore, that the dominant trend in recent years has been toward a social or cultural view of efficiency in those areas of knowledge and practice we have been considering.

Let us consider some of the ramifications of the social aspect of efficiency.

In the case of the individual producer, efficiency is the highest level of output for energy and talent expended. But the level of human efficiency here is probably as variable an aspect of the matter as any we might deal with. The multiple of causes which can produce waste as a result of individual action in the productive process is as numerous as the psychological and physiological variables affecting man. However, it seems safe to say that as an individual producer is socially well adjusted and as working conditions satisfy both physical and psychic well-being, then it is possible to maximize individual productive efficiency.[35] As a final qualification, it should be added that "highest level of output" is not always a quantitative measure with respect to either the individual or the process, for in many instances (perhaps most), quality is a far more important factor than mere quantification of units.

35. Suggested by Wallace H. Best in the unpublished thesis, above referred to.

As a citizen, the individual "is willing to accept not only a fair degree of chance but a fair degree of failure, provided that they appear to him to be the exception rather than the general rule."[36] But the means dominant in a society must be capable of bringing about a substantial realization of the basic beliefs and promises of that society.[37] Thus the individual as citizen insists on efficiency in terms of an adequate correlation between the theory and practice of the society in which he lives.

Efficiency for the individual personality is fundamentally the opportunity to realize its capacities to the utmost in every aspect of life. Naturally the ideal here is as limited as in all other forms of efficiency, due to opportunity, costs, and natural frictions. Nevertheless, if efficiency is to be achieved, the personality must be allowed to fulfill its potentialities in a ratio where satisfaction exceeds frustration, for it does not seem reasonable that a personality more wasted and thwarted than utilized and expanded can be thought of as efficient.

From the community or social viewpoint, efficiency combines many or most of the elements previously adverted to, plus some that have not heretofore been mentioned. Professor Walter J. Shepard, for example, in his presidential address to the American Political Science Association in 1934, analyzed the emerging "Philosophy of the Good Life," and included (1) the right of the worker to

36. Drucker, *op. cit.*, p. 135.
37. *Ibid.*, p. 134.

creative work; (2) the right to an adequate standard of living; and (3) the right to a substantial share in the management of the industry to which he has devoted his labor and his life."[38] His point of view coincides remarkably with that of Sumner Slichter, Harvard economist, in his book, *The American Economy, Its Problems and Prospects,* published in 1948, wherein is predicted a "laboristic" economy for the United States.

Ever since Elton Mayo, if not before, it has been widely realized that an important element of efficiency is giving the worker greater satisfaction on his job.[39] The modern idea is to give the employee a sense of importance and of "belonging" to the enterprise of which he is a producing part. Only in the last few years has this area been much studied and written about and it is not too much to expect that some of the largest gains in industrial and social efficiency will emerge from this fertile field.

Said one of my GI's who wrote a term paper on efficiency: "If American business and government are to keep the free enterprise system dynamic and meet the challenge of Communism and Socialism, it would behoove them to look much more thor-

---

38. *American Political Science Review,* Vol. XXVIII (Feb., 1934).
39. Elton Mayo, *The Human Problems of an Industrial Civilization* (original edition, New York, 1933; revised edition, Cambridge, Mass., 1946); and *The Social Problems of an Industrial Civilization* (Cambridge, Mass., 1945); F. J. Roethlisberger and W. J. Dickson, *Management and the Worker* (Boston, 1934); T. N. Whitehead, *Leadership in a Free Society* (Cambridge, Mass., 1936); F. J. Roethlisberger, *Management and Morale* (Cambridge, Mass., 1942); Stuart Chase, *Men at Work* (New York, 1945).

oughly into this subject of efficiency and particularly into this factor of human relationships."[40]

IV

Even if giant corporations were more efficient in an engineering, business, and managerial sense, as apparently they are not without qualifications, there would still be reasons of social efficiency causing some doubt as to the desirability of extending their size and number indefinitely. Several of these factors have been mentioned in previous essays, but suppose now we bring them together for a unified look.

The objections to corporate growth in excess of the clearly demonstrated needs of plant and engineering technology are principally three and relate to the economic, political, and social aspects of the matter. From an economic standpoint, excessive concentration may be the means of undermining the free market system in those areas where concentration is dominant, and eventually of undermining the entire system. The free market offers a better standard of efficiency, if allowed to operate through the law of supply and demand, the flexible allocation of resources determined by consumer demand, and a flexible price system, than the alternative method of judging efficiency under monopoly and socialism, namely, the use of statistical and managerial devices to determine the relative efficiency of units of enterprise of the same character. Price, of it-

40. John Penney, unpublished thesis above referred to.

self, if not always an adequate yardstick, but generally speaking it is a more reliable test, in the long run, than the comparisons of internal operating efficiency which must be relied on under monopoly conditions. In the free enterprise system, fortunately, both methods can be employed.

The second major objection to indiscriminate corporate growth is political. Excessive corporate concentrations engender national pressure groups which divide capital, labor, and agriculture sharply from each other. The inevitable tendency is to try to "capture" government and monopolize it instead of sharing it, as interests are content to do when all are relatively small and power is reasonably equally divided. The danger that this may happen increases in proportion to the aggressiveness of the contenders, for the power bloc that feels it is on the point of losing out may be tempted to use monopolistic methods relative to the control of government. And the final peril, if such a development occurs, is, of course, either fascism or communism. Short of either, there may be a growing demand for state socialism of some kind because when ownership is highly concentrated the average citizen is likely to conclude—as he apparently invariably has in other countries—that as between private and public monopoly he prefers the latter. Then, too, there is the lesser danger of weakening representative government if any interest becomes too powerful because of the money power which is theirs and the danger of buying elections and the media of mass communication.

Finally, there is the human or societal effect, which in many ways is the most important of the three but harder to explain in a way that does not suggest sloppy sentimentalism. An excess of corporate concentration limits the chances of owning one's own business, hence impedes the growth of personality referred to above. Standardization tends also to standardize the people who run the machines, robbing them of any color or individuality they might otherwise have had. This is what Brandeis feared most in bigness. It tends to make them deficient in resourcefulness, independence, and initiative, three of the most important traits of character supporting free enterprise and democracy. The over-all trend is toward oligarchy and elites, with a sharp line dividing the leaders from the led. These social losses are so great, and the desirability of retaining virtues such as independence and individuality so compelling, that some thoughtful individuals would trade a certain amount of machine efficiency, if necessary, in order to retain the spiritual and aesthetic values of our culture.

Nikolai Lenin once said, "The possibility of socialism will be determined by our success in combining the Soviet rule and the Soviet organization of management with the latest progressive measures of capitalism. We must introduce in Russia the study and the teaching of the New Taylor System and its systematic trial and adoption."[41] The USSR

41. "The Urgent Problems of the Soviet Rule," *Pravda*, April 28, 1918. Translated in *Bulletin of the Taylor Society*, Vol. 4 (June, 1919), pp. 35-37.

apparently sought efficiency. But efficiency for what? That is the question that the people of any nation should ask themselves.

Can we supply any fairly definite answers to the questions we have been raising? Let us try. First, as to the efficiency concept. Efficiency is a good and useful word and it will be a fortunate thing if the American people continue to emphasize it in the future. It is a strong, red-blooded word, conveying the notion of competence, skill, careful calculation. It is protection against the "cult of incompetence" which Walter Lippmann says may one day engulf us if we don't watch out.[42] But we should either give more attention than has been customary to a further broadening and humanizing of the term, if it is to cover all avenues and interests of life, or alternatively, we should try to use the term more precisely and give more thought to values other than efficiency and in addition thereto. The broadening process occurs gradually because usage, once established, changes slowly. The second alternative would therefore appear to be more feasible. The best plan, however, would be to attempt both—to give increasingly conscious thought to the implications of the term efficiency and at the same time reconsider the concept in a better weighted scheme of values in which efficiency, in some of its aspects, is deemphasized.

We need not agree with everything Ralph Bor-

42. "The Cult of Incompetence," *Today and Tomorrow*, (March 12, 1942, p. 21.

sodi says to concede that there is a grain of truth in his dire prediction. In his book, *This Ugly Civilization,* he describes the subtle but vicious encirclement of the efficiency mania: "New laws, new customs, new economic theories — which permit of greater coöperation, greater integration, greater efficiency — will take the place of those which prevail today. But efficiency will remain—to whip and drive and scourge the victims of this civilizaton."[43] The American concept of efficiency, said a prominent British writer fifteen years ago, is "machinelike in concept and inhuman in its operation." It is possible, of course, that he may have softened his judgment somewhat since then, because British industrialists now apparently realize that they have been slipping in efficiency, while at the same time, as we have seen, there has been a widening and humanizing of the concept in the United States.

If the definition of efficiency were broadened to conform to modern usage it might run something like this: Efficiency is the maximization of both the physical and the human values secured relative to the expenditures therefor, combined with the least amount of both physical and human waste. In these terms the definition of efficiency becomes a philosophy of political economy or even a cosmic philosophy.

On the other hand, if semantically it seems wiser to stick to a simpler definition, such as the highest level of output for energy and talent expended, no

43. Ralph Borsodi, *This Ugly Civilization* (New York, 1929), pp. 46, 49.

time should be lost in distinguishing additional values which need to be emphasized. Obviously these would be human, aesthetic, spiritual. National economic efficiency would involve quality as well as quantity, labor satisfaction as well as man-hour output, individual sharing as well as national power. Democracy, enlightenment, independence, and justice would be the goals of the political state and not merely economy and efficiency in the operation of the governmental institution. The ultimate test would be not how much production there is, in any and all realms, but how much of the good life all classes and segments of the population derive therefrom. In public administration, as well as in treatises on economics and business administration, this change in emphasis is fortunately already well advanced.

If the United States were to travel relentlessly down the road toward a collectivism primarily induced by an uncritically accepted growth of economic concentration, then it is doubtful whether a broadened and humanized concept of efficiency could be maintained in its essential vitality. And whether we shall be given the chance to restudy and reformulate the broader values here suggested will depend in large part, of course, on whether costly and destructive total wars can be eliminated, because today wars are becoming the chief stimulus to economic concentration and a main reliance of the would-be monopolist.

V

MANAGERIAL FREEDOM
AND THE ROLE OF GOVERNMENT

IF THE FREE ENTERPRISE system is to be maintained, government must be accorded greater authority than it now possesses to police corporate concentrations and to enforce competition. Government does not need a wider power; it needs more power to do a few essential things with reference to the economic system and do them well. What are these things? In broadest outline, to provide the security that the people are demanding.

But there are many ways of providing security, some of which strengthen and some of which weaken the competitive system and free enterprise. The need, therefore, is to formulate what Henry Simons calls a positive program for free enterprise which, in effect, means agreeing on the essential functions of government in the last half of the twentieth century. This is an inescapable task of responsible businessmen, and considering the heritage of hostile attitudes toward government that businessmen as a class have acquired, it will be a difficult and a precarious one. This process of reformulating the agenda of the state is equally incumbent on the lawmaker and the administrator, the latter of whom, in today's government, has so much influence relative to policy and purpose.

In America's quest for security, we must assure ourselves that initiative is safeguarded, and in our strong attachment to liberty we must not fail to differentiate between the things that government must do if a vital economy is to be maintained, and those things that are merely an opportunist collection of unrelated sidelines. Security is not having someone else take care of you: security is providing the conditions under which the individual can, through effort and if he chooses, provide the wherewithal to own his own means of securing a livelihood. Thus, security, like freedom, is both an individual and a community matter, for both depend for their continuance on the right balance of factors.

Insecurity is still America's Number One problem. In public concern, international tensions are followed closely by domestic economic problems, both of which create a sense of insecurity throughout the nation. According to a recent Gallup poll, economic problems (living costs, inflation, taxes) plus unemployment, strikes and labor troubles, and housing constituted 46 percent of the problems listed as the country's chief worries.[1] Only the complex of international concerns was mentioned more often. The problem is how to secure greater stability and still retain the values of our system, how to use government adequately and still keep it from discouraging voluntarism.

In the same Gallup poll, "corruption in government" was mentioned by only 3 percent as a prob-

1. Poll published May 5, 1950.

lem deserving major consideration, and hence, despite the attempt in some influential quarters to trace most of our troubles to government's door, apparently the effort has not been wholly successful. If this is correct, it is encouraging in view of the task ahead. Only when business and government learn to pull together in this country, each doing its appointed job and each staying within its proper sphere *made possible by the conditions existing at the time,* can we expect any long-range improvement in our fundamental sense of security.

We must stop talking like children and talk like responsible adults. Instead of falling back on analogies we must use factual descriptions. Instead of employing hopped-up emotional words, we should learn the value of simple ones encouraging reasonableness and clarity. The head of the California Medical Association to the contrary, government intervention is not "a great debilitating disease" and "a deadly infection."[2] It is a cause-and-effect relationship, due to discoverable pressures. These pressures invariably result from tensions in some segment of the population. All too often, unfortunately, what government does is not the perfect solution, but one of the chief reasons for this is that influential pressure groups, by their negativistic attitudes, make government a less effective instrument for solving our difficulties than it would otherwise be.

Alexander Leighton makes three points in the latter part of his book, *The Governing of Men,* that

2. *The Los Angeles Times,* May 1, 1950.

bear on the dangers inherent in continuing the essentially American practice of exaggerating the faults and berating the underlying necessity of our governmental system. These three points are stated in the form of principles or propositions. The first is that as systems of belief in a community under stress become more emotional, unstable, and conflicting, the community becomes less able to deal with the causes of stress. This is true of individuals, as all of us have observed, so why should it not be equally true of the community? The second proposition is that out of a community under stress there is likely to arise "a single radical system of belief" which may or may not bring a new stability, but which will give a large section of the population a sense of at least temporary relief from stress. By "radical" it is obvious that Leighton means extreme measures from either side of center and here again, the truth of the observation may be tested by applying it to individual situations where one "blows off steam" and feels temporarily better. Leighton's third and final proposition is that after a period of stress, when change has been rapid, there is a drift back toward former systems of belief, but the return is rarely, if ever, complete.[3]

It is extremes such as these that we should, if possible, try to avoid, and the first step is to use logic and eschew passion in discussing our common problems. The second is to think clearly and objec-

3. Alexander Leighton, *The Governing of Men* (Princeton, N. J., 1946), pp. 302-303.

tively. That this is all too rare today is seen in the wide range of current analyses and nostrums, all of which have some claim to credibility if convincingly enough presented. It is impossible that all of them should be valid because if the forces, factors, and psychological ingredients that are at work were correctly understood, the range of diagnosis and prescription would be in proportion to that found in other nonexact fields of science. If, as a result of developing better tools of analysis, we could reduce the range of variation, there is reason to believe that radical fluctuations could be avoided and the values of our system steadily maintained.

I

Brief reference to a group of popular books dealing with the role of government in the modern economy will help to show how wide the range of nostrums and prescriptions has become. John T. Flynn has written *The Road Ahead: America's Creeping Revolution* and thousands of copies have been circulated free by well-meaning businessmen and their associations. But despite the author's forensic skill (and perhaps also because of it), there can be no question that the book hinders rather than helps basic understandings and the solution of our most bothersome problems. Flynn does not get at the roots of difficulties. He does not study tensions to see what gave rise to them. He does not try to find out what various segments of the population are striving for, and why. He bases his whole argument on an incomplete set of assumptions: First, that government is a conspiracy against the free enterprise system with public officials the chief conspirators, and second, that no matter how little or how much governmental intervention various groups and individuals may think necessary, all such views are equally subversive of the American system of free enterprise. It is out of such oversimplified and extreme analyses that great mischief grows.

Flynn's particular devil he calls "Fabianism" and it is of British origin. The British Labour party, he says, began with the welfare state and moved in from there.[4] The United States is following the same road. British capitalism was destroyed by the loss of world trade after World War I and the adoption of Socialist social services. Welfare programs, he therefore argues, are a Trojan horse. The British Socialists early saw the immense value of social reform as a means of accustoming citizens to look to the state for the correction of all their ills; in this way, welfare agitation could be made the vehicle for imparting Socialist ideas into the minds of the common man. This statement portrays Flynn's argument as well as any. And on careful reading, what does one find? Is he opposed to all social reform? If not, does he think that the only reform justified is that which groups undertake without legislation or compulsion? Did the Fabians really recommend government solutions for "all"

4. John T. Flynn, *The Road Ahead* (New York, 1949), p. 24.

ills? What does the author mean by welfare "agitation"? Is this the same thing as proposed welfare legislation?

Flynn's basic error of logic is in assuming that mild measures inevitably produce radical results. This is true only if the mild measures are inadequate to the situation or if they come too late successfully to deal with the situation. Any practical man knows this is so. The experience of the medical practitioner in dealing with disease is in point.

But I have an idea that the difficulty goes even deeper. Flynn and the businessmen who agree with him seem to argue that human problems are regulated by preference and not, as in what they would call the real world (of business, for example), by cause-and-effect relationships. Those who assume such a difference themselves become divided personalities: in the business realm, thinking and logic operate; in government, only emotion and propaganda. But schizophrenia is doubly dangerous when applied to social solutions. It causes Flynn, for example, to attack moderates and liberals as being more dangerous than Communists, a conclusion he justifies by arguing that all of them, even without knowing it, are "Fabians" and Socialists. Liberals, Americans for Democratic Action, the Federal Council of Churches of Christ in America, organized labor, those who are concerned with the rights of Negroes and other minorities—all these Flynn lumps together indiscriminately and calls them subversive.[5]

5. *Ibid.*, Chaps. 5-10.

Flynn's language is intemperate. "These two systems," he says, "cannot live together in the same society."[6] What does he mean by this? They have lived together in the past. What kind of veiled threat is this for the future? Or another example of passion-arousing language; "It is one big war against our civilization."[7] Or this: "We must begin now to dismantle the tyrant State in America and to build up once again the energies of a free people."[8]

Flynn pays lip service to the free enterprise system and popular government but he seems to think that dogma and passion coupled with the condemnation of all liberals and reformers can save them. With many of his aspirations and beliefs there is general agreement amongst those that he blames for a growing collectivism. When he states, for example, that Americans should "build up once again the energies of a free people" or that we must stop apologizing for our capitalist system and appreciate it, liberals as well as conservatives respond fully and sincerely. But when he says that we cannot depend on any political party and that we must build a power outside parties so strong that parties will be compelled to yield to it,[9] one begins to doubt whether he is really attached to solutions achieved exclusively through democratic machinery or whether he is retreating from the American belief in free, representative government.

6. *Ibid.,* p. 151.
7. *Ibid.,* p. 154.
8. *Ibid.,* p. 160.
9. *Ibid.,* p. 158.

II

A position in marked contrast to Flynn's is taken by Seymour Harris and others who were once identified with the New Deal, in their book, *Saving American Capitalism,* published a year earlier than Flynn's *The Road Ahead.* Instead of arguing that government is the source of all collectivistic tendencies, they seek the causal factors of collectivism in the economy and in society itself. To them, government is affected by forces originating, for the most part, outside of government itself. Hence, unlike Flynn, they do not believe that the final outcome depends on a war of conflicting ideologies. They assume, rather, that when social tensions arise, voters will call on their governments to help find the solution unless voluntary agencies can find adequate solutions themselves.

Both a vigorous free enterprise system and an effective government are necessary if the economy is to be kept on an even keel, say these authors.[10] If either institution fails in its essential role, the free enterprise system is endangered. Instead of government's being the cause of our danger, therefore, its wise policies and efficient administration are a necessary condition to the survival of a free national economy. /How one thinks about the relation between government and the economy, therefore, is probably the most determinative factor in the saving of the American system. If realism and

10. Seymour Harris and Others, *Saving American Capitalism* (New York, 1948), p. 86.

a sweet reasonableness can be made more general, the sound instincts and tested energies of the American people can be relied on to preserve private ownership, competition, and managerial freedom.

What is the suggested test of governmental appropriateness? It is not fixed and unchanging, as in Flynn's analysis, but depends rather on time and circumstance. The more voluntary groups can do, the less government will be expected to do, and the more they fail, the more government will be asked to interfere and to operate. The test is pragmatic, not ideological. The way to keep government from doing too much is to analyze problems and to plan solutions far enough in advance of serious tensions that government's role may be held to a minimum.

A fundamental principle of political economy is enunciated at several points in the analysis in *Saving American Capitalism.* If a democratic nation is unprepared to accept *enough* government at any given time, so as to prevent disequilibriums from becoming aggravated, it will end up with *too much* government.[11] What at first blush seems to be a paradox proves on closer analysis to be a cause-and-effect theorem comparable to a law of physics. The reasoning is simple and convincing. If at any given time the government, for any reason, is allowed insufficient authority to maintain the essentials of the free enterprise system, such as effective compe-

11. See *Ibid.,* p. 23, for the clearest exposition of this principle.

tition, then unsolved difficulties will grow in severity and volume until at last, in the ensuing crisis, more will be demanded of government than would have been necessary if adequate steps had been taken at the appropriate time. A sense of timing is therefore of the essence. Every practical administrator knows how important a sense of timing is; what is not so widely recognized is that timing is equally essential in the formation of public policy.

The difficulty, as already suggested, is that most leaders of American business have one method of thinking for their own businesses and another system for their thinking about government. In their own business concerns they will tell you that of course prevention is better than cure, that when tensions occur something must be done to relieve them, and that an accurate sense of timing is one of the acid tests of a good administrator. But they seem to be unable to think in equally realistic terms when it comes to government. The reason for this is that emotionally they view government not as a part of the free enterprise system—and a vital part at that—but as something outside of and foreign to that system, as an enemy and not as an integral process.

The most important question in any age and in any society is the right relation between voluntary and collective activity. What determines the content of the private-public issue? Chance? Preference? Propaganda? None of these plays so important a role as realistic analysis. If for any reason private managers fail in the area of private decision-making, the government's role in the economy must surely increase. When in peacetime public authority is forced to invade the territory that should be set aside for private decision, then government controls will spread. One control will lead to another and the rate of increase will accelerate.[12] Here the principle of cumulation operates: Just as the growth of power in monopoly is cumulative, so the growth of control in government is cumulative. Moderate measures, long neglected, appear later as extreme remedies. Numerous tensions, left to themselves, burst forth as numerous controls. The greater the extent to which government is forced to manage the economy, the less of free areas is left for private managers and for the play of the free market system. The problem, therefore, is to see that such a state of affairs is avoided. All too often the conservative pins his hope on breast-beating and powerful invectives aimed at government. These have had, at best, but a partial and temporary success. The intelligent conservative will therefore change his tactics. For flag-waving he will substitute analysis, and for invective he will favor more effective decision-making to forestall the necessity of government controls. But before either is possible, a widespread change of attitude toward government, on the part of a large segment of American business, seems to be indicated.

12. *Ibid.*, p. 38.

An equally telling criticism may be made of many liberals. Flynn is undoubtedly correct when he says that some liberals pay only lip service to the advantages of the free enterprise system, rarely have a clear perception of what is involved in it, and sometimes appear to be insincere in their professed support of it. For this result, as remarked in the first essay in the present book, conservatives themselves are equally to blame, for relatively little attention has been given to making the tenets of the system explicit. Even admitting this, however, I cannot escape the conclusion that if the free enterprise system and popular government are to be maintained in the United States, it is as important for those associated with government to become well grounded in the elements of free enterprise as for businessmen to adopt a more intelligent self-interest toward government. The Economic Principles Commission of the National Association of Manufacturers pointed the way, in saying, "We could not have our present system of production and distribution without our present system of government, nor our present system of government without our present system of business. They are woven together like the threads in a piece of cloth, and anything that affects one part will alter the whole."[13]

In calling attention to the need for greater knowledge and appreciation of the free enterprise system on the part of those identified with government, I

13. *The American Individual Enterprise System*, 2 vols., (New York, 1946), I, p. 1.

do not mean to imply that the contributors to *Saving American Capitalism* are censurable in that regard. We favor capitalism, states the editor of the symposium, but are by no means assured that its future is secure. There is no ground for complacency. The depression was not over in 1938. A large part of the credit for recovery since that time is due to the demands of wartime production, to government guarantees, and to government planning. It is still up to us to prove that "capitalism is not but a passing phase in the historical process from feudalism to socialism."[14]

The program proposed by these authors for a "Second New Deal" must be read in its entirety to be fairly interpreted. None of the contributors must be understood as approving all the measures their colleagues advocate.[15] Some of the highlights of their economic positions, however, are these· America needs an "economic plan" or at the very least "an economic program for action";[16] business is entitled to full production and generous profits, but just as clearly, exorbitant profits are a threat to the health of our economy;[17] we may expect to enjoy prosperity only when the national income is high and when employment parallels the total na-

---

14. Harris, *op. cit.*, p. 4. Statements such as the last, which show the effect of the Hegelian-Marxist philosophy of history are, of course, seized upon by writers such as Flynn as evidence of noncapitalistic leanings.
15. Stated explicitly in the Editor's *Preface*.
16. *Ibid.*, p. 3.
17. *Ibid.*, p. 36.

tional demand for goods and services;[18] the most serious insufficiency in our previous antidepression efforts was that they did not place enough emphasis on restoring "balance within the enterprise system itself,"[19] and finally, when governments do too little they are invariably driven to do far too much in the end,[20] one inference from which is that governmental programming and administration must be continually strengthened if the enterprise system is to be faithfully served.[21]

III

The American economy is the most productive economy in existence, for, with about 6 percent of the world's labor force, it produces well over a third of the world's goods.[22] But despite its preeminence, the American economy "has great problems, and its institutions are under attack."[23] It is rapidly becoming a "laboristic" economy, says Sumner Slichter, in which the influence of employees is growing vis-a-vis that of management, and this trend may be expected to continue. The economy is said by some to be mature and to have lost much of its former ability to grow and expand; and at times it seems as though it is almost overwhelmed by the problems incident to a technological revolution.[24]

18. *Ibid.*, p. 234.
19. *Ibid.*, p. 85.
20. *Ibid.*, p. 169.
21. *Ibid.*, p. 86.
22. Sumner H. Slichter, *The American Economy* (New York, 1948), p. 3.
23. *Ibid.*, p. 4.
24. *Ibid.*, pp. 4-5.

Standing above all these issues, however, is the quest for security, the reconciliation of private freedom and public authority. Let us, therefore, try to bring together at this point some of the factors from which a salutary solution may be fashioned:

Security requires a better understanding of the free enterprise system and of its interrelatedness with popularly-controlled government.

Security entails a more widespread ownership of private property and of the means of obtaining a living by one's own efforts.

The common ingredient in free enterprise and in popular government is *shared* power.

The free enterprise system does not operate automatically. It involves concensus as to goals and as to values. It involves a high degree of self-restraint and of *noblesse oblige*. Its continued health requires an avoidance of excesses, whether they be exorbitant profits or totalitarian tendencies in government.

Welfare is not a luxury but a necessity. Social insurance is a foundation, not an extravagance. Health, security, education, and morals are pillars of national well-being, not a prop to the weak.

Sound security programs make use of positive measures of prevention, thus minimizing the need for costly outlays for poor relief and the unwitting encouragement of indolence.

A sound rule is for voluntary agencies—social and economic—to do everything that can be done on that basis, but not to hesitate to use government when private action is inappropriate or unsuccessful, or where human values can be promoted in no other way.

Security requires that ways be invented of keeping industry operating steadily without sharp ups and downs which destroy prosperity and cause large segments of the population to lose faith in the system that allows such calamities to occur.

The private ownership system makes competition a necessity. In a capitalistic society, when competition is endangered, the system itself is likely to break down.

Concentrated power, whether political, economic or ecclesiastical, is not compatible with free institutions. No man is good enough to be another man's master and even the good man who may become master stops being good in a very short time.[25]

Efficiency, broadly defined and interpreted, is a bulwark of any system. Efficiency, as an incentive, is the chief justification of profit-making.

A system of government regulation, soundly conceived and effectively administered, is thoroughly compatible with and strengthening to, the private enterprise system. Such government regulation should establish certain rules of the game and set certain acceptable standards of business performance, "without assuming the vital functions of business management."[26]

---

25. For an excellent statement of this position, see A. A. Berle, Jr., in Harris, *op. cit.*, pp. 43-44.
26. Moulton, *op. cit.*, p. 70.

Freedom of management, the third requisite of the free enterprise system and in many ways its capstone, would not be possible unless the other two were first assured.

If the creative power of private enterprise which has been responsible in large measure for the extraordinary industrial achievements of modern times is to be nurtured, then the chief role of government should be stabilization, not detailed control. One reason businessmen should take a more understanding attitude toward government is that only by such means, in all probability, will the necessary functions and priorities of the state relative to the total economy be determined in a manner compatible with the tenets of the enterprise system.

On balance, most people would probably agree with Sumner Slichter that "The American economy is a far better economy than most people realize."[27] Many, though possibly not as many, would also agree with him that in the "transformation of the American economy from a capitalistic to a laboristic society," there are, in the long run, probably more advantages than disadvantages to be expected.[28] One final matter of concern may be underscored. In listing ten possible factors on the "pessimistic" side of the ledger, Slichter mentions "The decline of the spirit of enterprise in the willingness of business managers to take chances."[29]

27. Slichter, *op. cit.*, p. 210.
28. *Ibid.*, pp. 213-214.
29. *Ibid.*, pp. 164-165.

IV

Which system is to predominate, free enterprise or the administrative state, will depend principally on how clearly the wielders of economic power come to understand what is involved. They help to make history—are not merely swept along by uncontrollable tides.

If periodically recurring wars and steady drifts toward economic concentrations are what is in store, then there is no question in my mind that socialism is the only end result that can be expected. Moreover, I am frank to admit that in consequence of having studied public ownership at close range, I am not as pessimistic about its efficiency as most businessmen apparently are, at least in their public statements. What I do not like about socialism is what I also object to in economic concentrations occurring under capitalism: the fact that power is not widely shared, that oligarchies are built up, and that individuality, although not impossible, is infinitely harder to secure.

If we are to steer clear of either extreme of collectivism, therefore, monopolistic capitalism on the one hand or state collectivism on the other, we must think more clearly than we have about the philosophy of the state, the economy, and the individual, and their juxtaposition in public policy and administration. In the preceding section certain guidelines were thrown out, some of them, admittedly, in the form that Stuart Chase would call unproved generalizations, or hypotheses requiring additional verification. I want here to add some concluding thoughts on the proper functions of government and the bearing they have on the main responsibilities of administrators for the future.

The proper functions of government are controlled only in part by preference; they are principally controlled by the extent to which the economy provides the conditions whereunder governmental service and intervention are either required or not required. Most businessmen in the United States, as a class, do not believe this to be so. They believe, rather, that if you have enough faith, then nothing you or anybody else does can change the essential character of the "system." In this naïve expectation they are almost certainly wrong. How much government is called upon to do and how free of outside interference the enterprise system is permitted to be, depend, as in the physical sciences, on forces and frictions, pressures and tensions, equilibriums and imbalances—in short, on the law of cause-and-effect. The human factor is relatively more important than in the physical sciences and humans are admittedly more unpredictable than ocean tides or atoms, but if we knew enough about human nature in relation to physical nature and social and economic institutions, we could greatly increase the accuracy of our predictions and, presumably, the prevention of many of our costliest social tragedies.

In the first essay it was shown how the free enterprise system is undergoing profound change in the United States, and is in danger of being lost, not because of an appreciable loss of emotional conviction but rather because world forces (principally war and preparation for war) and domestic forces (principally technology translated into social invention) force changes which are inadequately dealt with because inadequately understood. In the second chapter it was shown how bigness or giantism has become a main characteristic of our economic and governmental life. Some people are attracted by it while others (a greater number) dislike it and are anxious concerning its ultimate effects. It can hardly be claimed that anything approaching a rational and effective concensus has been attained, however, because, again, a knowledge of what to expect is not clearly enough documented and popular awareness, even of what evidence is available, is nowhere near enough appreciated.

In the third lecture it was observed that the solution often suggested for an overweening concentration of economic and governmental power is an increase of decentralization, primarily a managerial device, but it was suggested that possibly too much is expected from this remedy, that it is only one factor, and that there are others equally important. One of these is power, taking the form of domination and control. Another is the upsetting of power balances in society, leading to a threat of monopoly not only in the economic order but in the political state as well. A third factor is the nonmaterial values of a democratic system, for collectivism may succeed in producing large quantities of goods and services but at the price of diminished private ownership, individuality, and independence.

In the fourth discussion, it was shown how the concept of efficiency has become the justification relied on both in industry and in government for the bigness, standardization, and depersonalizing of relationships throughout the social fabric which we have allowed uncritically and somewhat complacently to come into existence; that a mechanical view of efficiency is not enough, and that if Americans wish to improve their culture, giving human factors foremost consideration, we must either broaden the definition of efficiency or accord greater weight to values which may be inconsistent with giantism and standardization.

Running through these four essays has been a recognition that events are controlled by a fine balancing of preference and causation, philosophy and science. In which case, the formulation of an adequate policy for the political economy would seem to require a more rounded and articulate philosophy of social dynamics on the part of our economic leaders and a greater awareness of economic values on the part of governmental leaders and administrators. Social dynamics is a knowledge of what causes change and what institutional and conceptual adjustments seem to be in order if the values of a given society are to be kept intact. It is this which constitutes the central storehouse of knowledge needed by our future captains of industry and our administrative statesmen.

With these considerations made clear, what, it may be asked, are the basic considerations regulating the ebb and flow of governmental functions? To serve human ends, to seek equilibrium, to avoid exceeding the optimum, and to respect time and circumstance; these are important benchmarks.

Human ends and nonhuman ends are hard to reconcile. When the individual or the institution seeks power merely for the sake of power, that is a nonhuman end; power is justified by its contribution to human betterment and freedoms. When the wielders of power seek size merely for the sake of size, that is a non-human end; size is justified by its effect upon human personality and opportunity. When leaders seek efficiency merely for the sake of efficiency, that is a nonhuman end; efficiency is justified only by its effect on people. When administrators seek the one best method, the resulting standardization is a nonhuman factor; administrative principle is justified only through consistency with cultural values which help all individuals as well as the administering institution.

Equilibrium is at once a goal of the economy and of the political state. When production equals effective demand there is likely to be well-being; when the power of management equals the power of labor there is likely to be a fair distribution of the national income; when all who are entitled to vote are allowed to vote there is likely to be peaceful change; when the authority at the center is balanced by the power at the periphery there is likely to be a better judgment and better coöperation; when the right balance is maintained between lawmakers and administrators there is likely to be the best balance of efficiency in government; and when the total power of a society is distributed between private and public agencies, all having essential jobs and none doing too much, there is likely to be greater efficiency and less danger of seizure of power by either.

The optimum for institutions, as for individuals, is the point at which the unit does its most effective job without undue strain on itself and without invading the corresponding rights of others. No one can do everything any more than any one person or institution can hope to possess everything. Nature intended it otherwise. To learn the point at which the law of diminishing returns sets in, therefore, and to be content with doing a better job in a smaller area than to seek a larger bailiwick and produce inferior results, is the beginning of wisdom for businessmen and lawmakers alike. If the champions of big business and big government were to believe this and act upon it, the free enterprise system and popular government might yet be saved.

Time and circumstance is not just a phrase. It is a basic factor in determining when government should interfere and when it should hold off. The conservative is wont to state that there are some things the government should never be allowed to do under any circumstances. The socialist contends that, given enough time, the government will do almost everything. Which is right? Neither, for the wisest statesmanship holds that government should do only what private enterprise cannot do as well or better, but that if private institutions fail and human values can be furthered in no other way, then government is justified in lending its assistance, hopeful that other institutions will improve their performance and permit it to withdraw. Since this is not a dogmatic position, it fails to satisfy many people and the interest groups. But it has the advantage of being scientific. Those who believe that time and circumstance are arbiters of power distribution recognize the underlying truth that social change is a matter of channeling wants and their fulfilment into institutional grooves which will do the most good and leave the least harm. They recognize that social responsibility and managerial competence go far toward determining who will eventually do the job. This makes for responsibility if not for changelessness, and for the dominance of human values and the subservience of vested interests, either governmental or business. If such a belief were fully accepted, the leaders of free enterprise would realize that they must either do their job, with full appreciation of what is involved in social responsibility, or someone else may have to do the job for them. This is a healthy state of affairs and a lesson which history amply justifies. On the obverse side, it means that government's functions must be kept under constant scrutiny, taking from it any duty that other institutions might perform as well or better. We sometimes overlook this part of the proposition because public administrators, like empire-building businessmen, often have voracious appetites.

The programs government will be responsible for in the future will likely emphasize security more than any other factor. Security is of two kinds, international and domestic. We shall need to find the means of guaranteeing peaceful settlements of international disputes and aggrandizements or the future of free enterprise and democracy appear black indeed. The load of debt may become so high that adequate profits and incentives will dry up at the source. The demands of total war may create conditions under which human values will be sacrificed to sheer power.

In the domestic realm, the role of government will probably expand in the direction of resource conservation, major regulation, social security, and planning. But if there were a wide appreciation of government in terms of prevention rather than cure, stabilization rather than direct operation, and balance rather than the furtherance of special interest, it might result in a reallocation of emphasis which would reduce the number of things government is required to do, while at the same time increasing the importance of what remains to be done. If planning were concentrated on the policies and means of strengthening competition and private ownership, there might be more freedom of management than is now prevalent. To fail to plan is to fail to take into account all the forces that produce social change planlessly. Planning of the right kind, in contrast, could result in a strengthening of the area retained by private ownership and management and a greater emphasis on those things that only government can do, at any time and under a particular combination of circumstances. This truth has been understood at least since the time of Jeremy Bentham and the Utilitarians, and is now increasingly emphasized by clear-thinking economists.[30]

If I were of an age where I was just preparing to enter the field of public administration, what assumptions would I make about those areas where the most needs to be done and where the greatest opportunities exist for profitable expenditure of effort? I would assume that the international field is the most important in terms of its eventual impact on human beings and human values. As a close second, however, I would recognize the strategic importance of the area we have been considering. Where economics and political science converge, there is found the field of political economy. It has to do with the institutions, processes, and motivations which together produce public policies administered by business and government leaders alike. Political economy is a quest for the principles of living that produce stability and the good life. Its end product is public policy, its instrument, administration.

I would also assume that political scientists should

30. See, for example, the convincing case made out by Henry C. Simons in *Economic Policy for a Free Society* (Chicago, 1948).

know more about economics and social pyschology and that economists should know more about political science and social psychology. I would emphasize policy equally with administrative methods and institutional life. I would, if possible, try to blend these ingredients and to bring them into an effective working accord. I would adopt a humanistic motif and make technical and machine efficiency subordinate to this test. I would emphasize the interchangeability of policy and administration, service as lawmaker and service as administrator. And, finally, although I would assiduously seek the secrets of group coöperation and smoothly functioning organization, I would at all times emphasize independence and self-reliance, for in this combination is found the working principle which gives vitality to free enterprise and free government.

Index

177